BUSTED

BUSTED

A Vietnam Veteran in Nixon's America

W. D. Ehrhart

Foreword by H. Bruce Franklin

University of Massachusetts Press / Amherst

"Guerrilla War" and "A Relative Thing," which appear in H. Bruce Franklin's foreword, were first published in *A Generation of Peace* (New York: New Voices, 1975) and are reprinted by permission of W. D. Ehrhart.

Copyright © 1995 by W. D. Ehrhart.
Foreword copyright © 1995 by H. Bruce Franklin.
All rights reserved
This book is published with the support and cooperation of
the University of Massachusetts Boston.
ISBN 0-87023-955-4(cloth)
LC 94-37563
Set in Adobe New Caledonia
Printed and bound by Thomson-Shore, Inc.

Library of Congress Cataloging-in-Publication Data
Ehrhart, W.D. (William Daniel), 1948-
    Busted: a Vietnam veteran in Nixon's America / W.D. Ehrhart;
foreword by H. Bruce Franklin.
      p.   cm.
ISBN 0-87023-955-4 (cloth: alk. paper)
1. Vietnamese Conflict, 1961-1975—Veterans—United States—Personal narrative.
I. Title
DS559.5.E37   1995
959.704'38—dc20   94-37563
                                CIP

British Library Cataloguing in Publication data are available

For Anne & Leela

Contents

Foreword

Among the hundreds of authors whose works I have assigned in dozens of courses at American public and private universities since 1961, I have never seen one have the same impact as W. D. Ehrhart. I have not even heard about any other author having the kind of effect I have witnessed.

In 1981 I began teaching a course called "Vietnam and America" at Rutgers University in Newark, an urban branch campus of New Jersey's state university attended mainly by working-class students. Two of the books that always seemed to generate enthusiastic responses were *Carrying the Darkness: The Poetry of the Vietnam War,* the splendid anthology edited by Ehrhart, and *Passing Time* (originally published as *Marking Time*), the second of his extraordinary autobiographical memoirs. So each year I used some of the modest funds available for lecturers to have Ehrhart come to the class to read his poems and discuss the war. But in 1993, when funds for lecturers disappeared (thanks to the financial crisis crippling public higher education), I was unable to invite him or any of the other Vietnam veteran authors who had generously shared their time with previous classes. When I walked into the classroom on the day *Passing Time* was due, there was a strange hubbub. One very bright, articulate, and conservative young man, who had attended a military school and was planning to be a career military officer—and who had been arguing vociferously with me all semester—seemed especially upset. Suddenly he blurted out:

"I've never read a book like this. It's changing my whole life." The next thing I knew, he was up in front of the class saying, "We've got to have this guy come talk with us. Why don't we kick in to get whatever it takes to bring him." There was a chorus of assent. Someone called out from the back, "Let's each put in five dollars." Someone else yelled, "five dollars? It costs seven fifty just to see a movie." "OK," said a new voice, "let's make it ten dollars." And so most of these students, almost all of whom work at least part time to be able to afford tuition, contributed ten dollars apiece to get a visit from W. D. Ehrhart.

When Ehrhart came, the student who had led this spontaneous movement made the introduction and then handed him the bundle of cash. In characteristic style, Ehrhart said later that this money meant more to him than any he had ever received in his life. His lecture was, as always, electrifying, and he had to be almost literally torn away from students still hanging on his every word over an hour after the class officially ended.

This was one of the most thrilling experiences I have had in my decades as a teacher. But it was also puzzling. For if these working-class students, a heterogeneous mix of America's urban and suburban ethnic groups, responded with such fervor to Ehrhart's writing, why were his books not selling in the hundreds of thousands? These were no elite or coterie readers, but ordinary Americans representing a vast potential audience. Ehrhart's relative obscurity on America's literary landscape could hardly be explained by any loss of interest in the Vietnam War and the literature generated by it. Literature by Vietnam veterans has been especially honored and well received: Larry Heinemann's *Paco's Story* won the National Book Award in 1987. Robert Olen Butler's *A Good Scent from a Strange Mountain* received the 1993 Pulitzer Prize for fiction. The 1994 Pulitzer Prize for poetry went to Yusef Komunyakaa. David Rabe's plays have won the Obie Award, Drama Desk Award, Drama Guild Award, and New York Drama Critics Circle Award. Joe Haldeman's *The Forever War* has sold more than a million copies. Ron Kovic's 1976 autobiography *Born on the Fourth of July* went through numerous printings even before Oliver Stone translated it into the 1989 hit movie—though it is worth noting that some scenes in the film (such as the college sequence) seem based more directly on Ehrhart's *Passing Time* than on anything in Kovic's powerful book in the same genre.

Among those who professionally study and teach Vietnam War literature, Ehrhart is admired at least as much as any of these justly celebrated writers. Some consider him the preeminent figure in this literature—treasured for his nonfiction, enormously influential as the foremost anthologist of Vietnam War poetry, and himself unsurpassed as a poet. A few days after the lecture sponsored by my students, I attended a major three-day conference, "The United States and Viet Nam: From War to Peace" held at Notre Dame in early December 1993. Among the dozens of sessions, plenaries, talks, and readings, including Pulitzer Prize and National Book Award winners, one and only one presentation received a standing ovation: a poetry reading by W. D. Ehrhart. This is surely an example of unequivocal peer recognition.

Ehrhart does have a following, one that is devoted, enthusiastic, and steadily growing. His poems are gradually finding their way into literature anthologies and high-school textbooks. The profundity of his prose is becoming recognized. But why is he not a household name among the serious reading public?

Part of the problem may be in Ehrhart himself. Some of the very qualities that make him such a potent writer—his passion, searing honesty, and scorn for greed, duplicity, pettifogging, selfishness, bureaucracy, and the self-serving ethos of the corporate world—make him an inept businessman, particularly unsuited for success in these tough times for serious authors in the U.S. publishing industry. Not one of his four previous books of nonfiction has had an appropriate publisher or been published in the trade format required for attention in the major review media. They have appeared only as mass-market paperbacks (a form rarely reviewed) or as publications of McFarland & Co., a very good but tiny niche publisher of specialized reference texts. McFarland licensed his first nonfiction book, *Vietnam-Perkasie*, to a mass-market house, which put it out as a paperback aimed at the thrill-seeking readers of survivalist military adventure stories. With the kind of irony appropriate to Ehrhart's career, the cover pictured him as a gung-ho Marine "toting an M-16 in the jungles of Vietnam" in front of a billowing U.S. flag. But the main explanation for Ehrhart's relative obscurity lies elsewhere.

Vietnam-Perkasie: A Combat Marine Memoir actually is basic to understanding Ehrhart's life and the trajectory of his succeeding three autobiographical memoirs: *Passing Time: Memoir of a Vietnam Veteran Against the War*; *Going Back: An Ex-Marine Returns to Vietnam*; and the present volume. It is a stunning chronicle of how a red-white-and-blue American boy from the model American small town—"where people left their homes unlocked at night" and "carolers strolled from house to house on Christmas Eve"—is transformed by the Vietnam War into a human powder keg filled with an explosive mixture of rage and guilt and shame about himself and his country. This is the book that gives the most complete account of Ehrhart's experience in the war itself, opening with his physical wounding in the ferocious 1968 battle to retake the city of Hue and closing with scenes back in the United States that dramatize his psychological wounding. The main narrative is an extended flashback that takes him from his upbringing in that idyllic Pennsylvania town of Perkasie and his ultrapatriotic enlistment in the U.S. Marines at age seventeen through boot camp, the nightmare of discovering his identity as an unwanted invader, a murderer, and an instrument of imperial policy in Vietnam, and his return to an America that has become for him an alien place. This is a familiar story in the literature by Vietnam veterans, similar to that told as brutally realistic autobiography in Kovic's *Born on the Fourth of July*, as the sometimes surreal fiction of Tim O'Brien and Larry Heinemann, or as interstellar science fiction in Haldeman's *The Forever War*. *Vietnam-Perkasie* features one characteristic of Ehrhart's writing that distinguishes it from most, though not all, literature by Vietnam veterans (or anybody else)—he reveals things about his own actions that very few of us are brave enough to disclose. As he relentlessly probes the moral significance of these actions in Vietnam, moreover, he begins to display their historical significance. This leads to what is most distinctive about *Vietnam-Perkasie*, Ehrhart's ability to shape the autobiographical memoir into his own recognizable brand of vehicle for exploring history through personal experience.

Even as a high-school student, Ehrhart was committed to the belief in a crucial relationship between American history and the role of each individual American. It was this belief that led him in 1964 at the age of sixteen to ride around Perkasie on the back of a flatbed truck "singing Barry Goldwater campaign songs" for he was "fed up with Lyndon Johnson and his refusal to stand up to the communists in Vietnam." *Vietnam-Perkasie* reprints his 1965 high-school editorial filled with detailed historical arguments supporting the U.S. role in the Vietnam War and concluding with this rebuke to those who say that Americans are "dying for no good reason" in Vietnam: "What more noble a cause can a man die for, than to die in defense of freedom?" A few days after writing this, he decided to enlist in the Marines so that he could fight in Vietnam to defend freedom and his country.

By describing in undiluted detail what he actually experienced in Vietnam, *Vietnam-Perkasie* presents the raw materials from which Ehrhart was to fashion most of his early poems. Like many other Vietnam veteran poets, he developed a strikingly plain style, remarkable for its concision and avoidance of the mannerisms that have made "poetry" seem like a coterie activity. For example, in the sixty-five words that constitute the poem "Guerrilla War," Ehrhart dramatizes the basic facts of life for U.S. ground troops in Vietnam, facts that demolish the entire argument of his patriotic high-school editorial:

> It's practically impossible
> to tell civilians
> from the Vietcong.

Nobody wears uniforms.
They all talk
the same language,
(and you couldn't understand them
even if they didn't).

They tape grenades
inside their clothes,
and carry satchel charges
in their market baskets.

Even their women fight;
and young boys,
and girls.

It's practically impossible
to tell civilians
from the Vietcong;

after a while,
you quit trying.

If one had to choose a single brief text to teach the history of the
U.S. war in Vietnam, could one do better than Ehrhart's "A Relative Thing"?

We are the ones you sent to fight a war
you didn't know a thing about.

It didn't take us long to realize
the only land that we controlled
was covered by the bottoms of our boots.

When the newsmen said that naval ships
had shelled a VC staging point,
we saw a breastless woman
and her stillborn child.

We laughed at old men stumbling
in the dust in frenzied terror
to avoid our three-ton trucks.

We fought outnumbered in Hue City
while the ARVN soldiers looted bodies

in the safety of the rear;
the cookies from the wives of Local 104
did not soften our awareness.

We have seen the pacified supporters
of the Saigon government
sitting in their jam-packed cardboard towns,
their wasted hands placed limply in their laps,
their empty bellies waiting for the rice
some district chief has sold
for profit to the Vietcong.

We have been democracy on Zippo raids,
burning houses to the ground,
driving eager amtracs through new-sown fields.

We are the ones who have to live
with the memory that we were the instruments
of your pigeon-breasted fantasies.
We are inextricable accomplices
in this travesty of dreams:

but we are not alone.

We are the ones you sent to fight a war
you did not know a thing about.
Those of us that lived
have tried to tell you what went wrong.
Now you think you do not have to listen.

Just because we will not fit
into the uniforms of photographs
of you at twenty-one
does not mean you can disown us.

We are your sons, America,
and you cannot change that.

When you awake,
we will still be here.

The qualities that characterize *Vietnam-Perkasie* and Ehrhart's
poetry—the distinctive flat voice speaking in a deceptively plain
style, the painful honesty and insights, the visceral power, the rare

fusion of personal and historical vision—also drive his later prose narratives and make them identifiable as uniquely his own. On the surface, each narrative seems fairly straightforward, but closer inspection reveals that Ehrhart is following the classic dictum that the greatest art lies in the concealment of art.

This, I think, is why *Passing Time* hits my students so hard. There seem to be no aesthetic pretensions here, just the apparently simple story of how an idealistic gung-ho seventeen-year-old joins the Marines, fights in Vietnam, returns to an alien nation, and then goes through a series of ever-more devastating discoveries about himself and America. Published in 1986, the narrative begins and ends in 1974 with Ehrhart, a lowly engine-room seaman on an oil tanker, playing casino with an engineer named Roger. The story seems loosely constructed, returning intermittently to these card-playing scenes, with Roger serving as interlocutor, audience, and foil for Ehrhart, who believes he is burnt out but who is really smoldering and rumbling like a dormant volcano ready to blow its top. Actually there are four narrative frameworks. first is the 1986 book itself, a construct of its thirty-eight-year-old author. Inside this is the enclosing narrative, the 1974 tanker episodes about the twenty-five-year-old Ehrhart. Within this unthreatening framework, Ehrhart recounts his excruciating discoveries as a veteran in the critical years beginning in 1969. The narrative of those five years serves as a third container, through which his most traumatic experience, that in Vietnam, bursts through as flashbacks. Emphasizing his own naïveté and ignorance, Ehrhart the narrator successfully conceals until late in the book Ehrhart the author's relentless engagement with history, which is woven into the camouflaged intricacies of the narrative with covert subtlety and sophistication.

The most crucial scene comes during the 1970 invasion of Cambodia when Ehrhart, now a Swarthmore student, broods by himself instead of going with his girlfriend, Pam, to a campus antiwar meeting and then, in a guilt-ridden rage, brutally punches her when she returns. As she "lay there staring up at me with a look of abject, naked, raw terror in her eyes," the narrator confronts a hideous truth about himself:

Oh, God almighty, what have I done? Here it was, here it was at last: Pam's eyes were the same eyes I'd seen in a thousand faces in a hundred villages, staring up at me in mute hatred as I towered over her, my whole body still cocked, ready to explode again. And this time there was no rifle, no uniform, no Sergeant Taggart barking orders, no mines, no snipers, no grenade ready to explode, no juggernaut momentum of a vast military bureaucracy out of control and bogged down in human quicksand, not a single excuse with which to defend myself.

So this is what you are, I thought.

Although he begs forgiveness, Pam expels him from her room, and he drinks himself into oblivion. When he awakes late the next afternoon, it is to a voice on the radio: "students wounded, at least four killed." He finds a newspaper headlined "Four Students Killed at Kent State":

One of the photographs accompanying the article showed a line of national guardsmen on the crest of a low hill. Another showed a young woman kneeling on the ground, her mouth twisted open in a scream, her face contorted with rage and anguish and shocked disbelief, her eyes swollen with tears, her arms outstretched toward the corpse of a man lying facedown in a pool of blood.

It was a photograph of Pam. Pam! And look there! Among the soldiers! That's me! The third one on the left! No!

After crying uncontrollably "until there was nothing left inside," he says that "my mind was more lucid than it had ever been before." The scene is so poignant and painfully revelatory that it is easy to miss the complex mixture of insights and illusions—both personal and historical—of its concluding words:

And then I knew. It was time—long past time—to put aside excuses and pride and vain illusions. Time to forget all that was irretrievably lost. Time to face up to the hard, cold, utterly bitter truth I'd tried to avoid for nearly three years. The war was a horrible mistake, and my beloved country was dying because of it. America was bleeding to death in the ricefields and jungles of Vietnam, and now the blood flowed in our own streets.

> I did not want my country to die.
> I had to do something.
> It was time to stop the war.
> And I would have to do it.

The author's awareness of his narrator's self-deception comes across most clearly in the tragicomic final line, where the movie-inspired heroic self-image and idealistic patriotism that had motivated Ehrhart the high schooler to volunteer to win the war now persuades Ehrhart the veteran that he should and can stop the war. John Wayne will now be a lone hero for peace. As the narrator goes on, he is forced to confront his personal limits and the illusions of his male ego. But far more agonizing are his confrontations with historical illusions and deception.

"The war was a horrible mistake," Ehrhart concludes amid his brutalization of Pam and the killings at Kent State. If my students are at all representative, many readers at this point get taken in. Because the scene is so painfully revelatory, we are not tempted to question the accuracy of this conclusion. Besides, in the 1980s and 1990s we are now supposed to believe that this was the essence of the antiwar position: "The war was a horrible mistake." Widely promulgated in the form of the "quagmire" metaphor developed by David Halberstam, it has become a kind of orthodoxy, offered as the liberal alternative to the right-wing view of the Vietnam War as—to use Ronald Reagan's phrase—"a noble cause." But unlike his narrator in 1970, the author of *Passing Time* does not believe that the Vietnam War was a "mistake," and he is tricking us into sharing his 1970 view in order to shatter it more effectively.

One year (and twenty chapters) later, Ehrhart—like millions of other Americans in 1971—encounters the *Pentagon Papers*, unassailable proof that the war was no "mistake," no "quagmire" into which America's leaders had unwittingly stumbled, but the product of elaborate secret plans and byzantine official deceit:

> A mistake? Vietnam a mistake? My God, it had been a calculated, deliberate attempt to hammer the world by brute force into the shape perceived by vain, duplicitous power brokers. And the depths to which they had sunk, dragging us all down with them, were almost unfathomable.

Passing Time then condenses with terrific concision the core of the *Pentagon Papers*, the U.S. government's top-secret history of its war against Vietnam, as the outraged responses of the young man who had mistakenly thought he had lost all his illusions a year earlier. "Here were," as the narrator puts it, in "the government's own account": Colonel Edward Lansdale's sabotage teams, infiltrated into Vietnam "even before the 1954 Geneva accords"; the creation of the U.S. puppet dictatorship of Ngo Dinh Diem; the Eisenhower administration's prevention of free elections; the secret dispatch of combat units by the Kennedy administration in 1961; the "U.S. government's direct connivance in the overthrow of Diem"; "the secret commando raids against North Vietnam"; "the plans for bombing the north more than a year before they were executed, the power brokers waiting, waiting for the chance, the excuse, some pretext the American people would believe"; "the evidence that the years of negotiations and temporary bombing halts had been no more than public-relations ploys designed to dupe the American people into supporting the ever-increasing escalation of the war" right on through 1971. *The Pentagon Papers* demonstrates to Ehrhart that from the beginning the war had been planned and executed by "a pack of dissembling criminals who'd defined morality as whatever they could get away with," "a bunch of cold-blooded murdering liars in three-piece suits and uniforms with stars" who "sent the children of the gullible halfway around the world to wage war on a nation of peasant rice farmers and fisherpeople." Like the American nation as a whole, Ehrhart had wanted to believe that the war was a "mistake," for the alternative, now forced upon him, is far more horrifying to face:

> I'd been a fool, ignorant and naive. A sucker. For such men, I
> had become a murderer. . ,. . For such men, I had been willing to
> lay down my life. And I had been nothing more to them than a
> hired gun, a triggerman, a stooge, a tool to be used and discarded,
> an insignificant statistic. Even as the years since I'd left Vietnam
> had passed, even as the doubts had grown, I had never imagined
> that the truth could be so ugly.

Reading passages like this, one realizes that Ehrhart's relative obscurity is not merely—or primarily—a product of his lack of business acumen or his bad luck in publication. As Ehrhart is acutely aware, the message at the heart of his poetry and prose is one that the "power brokers" certainly do not want the nation now to hear or remember. Because men like these control corporate publishing and the major media, one would have to be a bit naive to expect Ehrhart's works to be widely ballyhooed.

Busted: A Vietnam Veteran in Nixon's America, which picks up where *Passing Time* left off, is immediately recognizable as an Ehrhart narrative: it is about an all-American guilt-ridden Marine Vietnam veteran discovering through brutally honest confrontation with himself devastating insights into the society that produced him; its surfaces seem simple and straightforward enough; it's a page turner. A reader familiar with *Passing Time* can detect right away some of Ehrhart's characteristically sly strategies for weaving history into the story, especially the outraged and enraged narrator battering his friends with his insights while their rejoinders highlight his quixotism. Ehrhart puts some of the sharpest insights into his own foibles and follies in the mouths of others, especially lawyer Richards, who tells the narrator, "Sometimes I think you want to make your life as hard as you can. . . . If you can't find something to be angry about, you just keep pushing until you do." But there is more going on here than meets the eye, for *Busted* is more artistically complex than any of Ehrhart's earlier narratives. Indeed, the title itself has more meanings than a New Critic could find in a metaphysical poem.

On one level, this is a simple story of how the narrator got "busted" for possession of marijuana while working as a seaman, how this busted his life, and how in an *Alice-in-Wonderland* trial he busted the attempt to take away his seaman's card. The triviality of his offense and of the trial itself is played off against the real crimes that have busted the narrator's identity: "I'm guilty, all right. I'm guilty of murder, attempted murder, arson, assault and battery, aggravated assault, assault with a deadly weapon, robbery, burglary, larceny." These are crimes that he believes he committed in Vietnam, crimes for which he was given medals by the same government that is now persecuting him for possession of a small amount of pot. From these contradictions Ehrhart spins a complex web of relations between the narrator's experiences in Vietnam and in America, before and after. *Busted* also features a second major character, who, although he never appears in person, lurks everywhere as the nemesis of the narrator: Richard Nixon.

As the narrator's ludicrous little trial is put off and on again over a period of months, President Nixon is simultaneously becoming ever more entangled in the Watergate web and thus being exposed as a far more dangerous criminal than the narrator. The parallels become increasingly ironic until, on the very day when the narrator is acquitted of the pot possession charge, Nixon, having been busted from the White House, is pardoned by Gerald Ford, his appointed successor, of any and all crimes he may have committed while president.

This ingenious structuring produces continual flashes of insight, like lightning bolts between oppositely charged bodies. Ehrhart's most audacious innovation, however, lies in still another dimension, added by the presence of "ghosts" of three friends killed in Vietnam. Combining elements of chorus, interlocutor, conscience, and dark comedy, the voices of the dead have the final words of the narrative. These words are, ironically, the most optimistic in

Busted, and they leave the narrator pointing forward to his future life as the artist who will design the work the ghosts inhabit. *Busted* thus concludes as a kind of nonfictional bildungsroman, or portrait of the artist as young man discovering the life determined for him by being busted.

Ehrhart here uses to great advantage that wonderful ability to condense history and unobtrusively display its relevance to everyday life. The book weaves in a pithy history not just of the Vietnam War and the Nixon saga but also of the revealing relations between the legalization of alcohol and criminalization of marijuana. The immense fissures fracturing American society during the early 1970s, symbolized in the Nixon saga and the pot trial, are dramatized in the confrontations between Vietnam veterans and the forces of law and order, especially in several scenes where the narrator is busted by gun-wielding cops for the crime of his counterculture appearance.

Because of its tricky narrative structure and daring use of ghosts, *Busted* may not please all admirers of Ehrhart's earlier prose works and may be more susceptible to misinterpretation. Nevertheless, it is a fascinating and original work that offers new evidence of what an important contemporary American author we are privileged to have in W. D. Ehrhart.

As this introduction was being drafted, *Busted* took on added significance with the death of Richard Nixon and his resurrection as a "genius" of foreign policy who "inherited the Vietnam War in 1968" (in the words of several AP stories and numerous editorials in the last week of April 1994) and successfully negotiated its end, as we were informed by a media blitz. His tombstone reads: "Richard Nixon, 1913-1994. The greatest honor history can bestow is the title of peacemaker."

The truth, which informs *Busted* as well as *Passing Time* and many of Ehrhart's poems, is that Richard Nixon as vice president was one of the principal architects of the Vietnam War, and that as president he conspired for four years to keep the war going, finally ending it in 1973 on terms that were less favorable to Washington than those offered by his Vietnamese opponents in early 1969. In April 1954, before the fall of Dien Bien Phu and before the opening of the Geneva conference that ended the French war against Vietnam, Vice President Nixon publicly declared that because "the Vietnamese lack the ability to conduct a war by themselves or govern themselves," in the event of a French withdrawal "the Administration must face up to the situation and dispatch forces." Within two months, as Ehrhart later learned from the *Pentagon Papers*, the Eisenhower-Nixon Administration had set up the Diem dictatorship and dispatched the first U.S. covert-action teams.

W. D. Ehrhart was then six years old. He had no way of knowing that the U.S. war in Vietnam had begun, much less the role it was to play in his life. Nor was Richard Nixon aware of the existence of Bill Ehrhart or of how their lives would intersect.

When the men in the White House and the Pentagon made the decision to send Americans to fight in Vietnam, they probably never gave a thought to the literature that might be produced by the U.S. veterans of what we now call the Vietnam War. How would these men have responded if someone had whispered in their ears that this literature would constitute one of the few great American achievements of that war? Or that maybe, someday, this literature will help us recognize the difference between a Richard Nixon and a Bill Ehrhart, that is, the difference between a warmaker and a peacemaker?

H. BRUCE FRANKLIN
May 1, 1994

Preface

In order to protect the privacy of living persons and the families
and relatives of the dead, I have changed the names of most people
in this book, except for those of obvious public figures.

I am indebted to Bruce Franklin, Barbara Tischler, and Paul
Wright for the trouble they've gone to on my behalf; to Robbie
Franklin and Rhonda Herman of McFarland & Company for their
patience and loyalty; and to Jan Barry for allowing me to excerpt
lines from his poem "Viet Nam," the full text of which can be
found in *Demilitarized Zones: Veterans After Vietnam*, Jan Barry
and W. D. Ehrhart, eds. (East River Anthology, 1976).

W. D. Ehrhart
Philadelphia
June 1994

BUSTED

I WAS SCARED SHITLESS the morning my cabin door banged open and Captain Henry Kyle blew in. Close behind him, sucked along by the force of his righteousness, came the chief engineer, the radio officer, the bosun, the company's union chairman, three company executives in gray business suits, and a man in street clothes I'd never seen before. The cabin became very crowded very quickly. I was sitting bolt upright before I knew it.

Captain Kyle glared down at me. He was a tall, angular man pushing seventy, with a shock of white hair and ramrod posture. He'd spent his entire life at sea, half of it as a ship's master. His eyes burned, as though the lookout up in the crow's nest had just hollered, "There she blows! There she blows! A hump like a snow-hill! It is Moby Dick!"

In the flicker of a ship cat's whisker, I thought about bolting for the door. Nine men blocked the way. The thought vanished, as if it had never existed. I lay back and waited for my stomach to splatter against the bottom of the dark vertical shaft through which it was falling.

"Get dressed," Kyle commanded in his low southern drawl. I threw back the sheet and stood up. I was naked. The captain and the chief engineer and the radio officer and the bosun and the union chairman and the three company executives and Mister X

1

stood there staring at me while I got dressed.

"Wait outside," Kyle commanded. I stepped through the hatchway. The bosun followed me. The rest of the search party stayed behind. I leaned against the bulkhead a few yards down the passageway. The bosun leaned against the opposite bulkhead, facing me.

"Got a cigarette, Dutch?" I asked.

"No," he said. There was a pack of Lucky Strikes in his breast pocket. I could see the bright red circle against a white background through the fabric of his shirt. My knees kept wanting to buckle. My body kept wanting to slump to the deck, but I forced myself to stay upright. Like moving down a jungle trail, the Viet Cong nowhere and everywhere in the darkness.

Captain Kyle emerged from my cabin, his humorless minions in tow. "Wait inside," he commanded. I went back inside. Someone banged the door shut behind me. The cabin had been ransacked. Drawers stood open, the contents disheveled and strewn about. The locker doors stood open. Even the mattress had been turned upside down and stripped.

I opened the door a crack. Dutch was still standing in the passageway. I could hear the search party rattling around in the cabin next door. I went over to the porthole and looked out. Then I opened the porthole, stuck my head and one arm out, and started banging on the hull. "Wake up!" I hollered, trying to do it discreetly. "Wake up. Jake. Hey, Jake. Wake up. Are you there, Jake?" In a few moments, the porthole directly above mine swung open. Jake poked his head out and looked down.

"What the fuck?" he said sleepily.

"We're getting raided," I said. "Captain Kyle just turned my cabin upside down. He's in Scotty's cabin now. You better get the word out." I pulled my head back in and closed the porthole, then went over to my bunk, replaced the mattress and sat down. Holy fuck, I thought, I'm going to prison. I'm duckshit.

After years of looking, I had finally found a place where I belonged. I was going to spend the rest of my life floating around on the margins of the world. They couldn't touch me here, I'd thought. Now it was gone in the snap of a tripwire. Nowhere was safe.

I'm duckshit. I knew I had to do better than that, but it's all I could think of. Like walking toward an ambush, awash in a sea of adrenaline, wanting to be anywhere but here and knowing there is nothing for it but to keep walking, forcing the body to do what it must, forcing the mind to work.

They would have to give me one phone call. At least they were supposed to. I thought of Jack Gold. His father was a business-man who owned half of northern California, a man with connec-tions. If anyone could get me a good lawyer, he could. I found Gold's phone number in my address book, wrote it down on a separate piece of paper, and slipped it down my sock. Then I be-gan to straighten up the cabin and pack my seabag.

It took me a long time. The air in the cabin had become heavy, almost viscous. It felt as if I were wading through deep sand. First, I folded the sheets and blankets on the bed. Then I emptied out the wall locker, carefully folding each piece of clothing before rolling it into a tight knot and stuffing it into the seabag the way I'd learned in boot camp almost eight years earlier.

That first night at boot camp in June 1966 had been the most terrifying experience of my life: drill instructors screaming death threats in your face from a distance of three inches while banging on garbage can lids; scared kids who'd started that day in the com-fort of their own kitchens back on the block awkwardly writhing this way and that in a formation known as asshole-to-bellybutton, a human worm, huge, tripping over each other's feet, stripped naked and reclothed in stiff green dungarees ten sizes too big, heads shaven clean as eggshells under bare light bulbs shining off skin so white it hurt your eyes, and the brain full of fear.

Later, even in the worst of the fighting, you could always grip your rifle for comfort and hunker down inside your flak jacket and helmet and hope the big stuff landed on somebody else's head while you prayed to that magic number that was your rotation date back to the World. But that first night at Parris Island, there was nothing to fight back with and nowhere to hide from those relentless DIs. I had never imagined men so mean or hard or angry. And they didn't want me in their Marine Corps. I was having second thoughts myself, but it was too late for that. "You're going to die on this island," they had said. I believed them.

It had all been smoke and mirrors, finally. It had been their job to frighten me. They were trying to prepare me for the rigors of battle. I was seventeen years old, and the worst battle I'd ever been in had resulted in a bloody nose. But I was hellbent on going to Vietnam because Lyndon Johnson had said that if we didn't stop the communists in Vietnam, we would one day have to fight them on the sands of Waikiki, and that sounded pretty damned serious to me. The DIs had done their job as well as anyone could have. Luck had kept me alive in Vietnam, but the DIs had kept me from losing my mind. Just the same, the memory of that first night could still wrench me out of sleep, bug-eyed and shivering in the darkness.

But this was worse. Much worse. This wasn't smoke and mirrors. There was no graduation day to look forward to, my parents up in the reviewing stand beaming proudly while their son paraded past, a perfectly disciplined Marine in a well-oiled platoon of eighty new Marines who could march as if they were one. There was no rotation date to pray to, knowing that if you were still alive on that magic day, they would put you on the Freedom Bird and send you back to the World. I hadn't volunteered for this. The men who had raided my cabin did not scream or shout or threaten. These men were sober. They had gone about their business with the cold determination of priests intent upon stamping out a heresy. They were not the least bit concerned for my survival. They meant to put me away.

I had never heard anything nice about prisons. They were dark, evil places where men without hope or mercy raped each other and stabbed each other and defecated in toilets without seats. I was only five feet, seven inches tall, 140 pounds, and I didn't know karate or judo or kung-fu. At least in Vietnam, I'd had a rifle. I'll die in prison, I thought. I'll never survive that. I don't want to try. I'd rather die now. I could hear the muffled sounds of the search party farther down the hall, rooting and clawing through someone else's cabin.

I turned to start packing up the stuff in the desk and nearly jumped out of my skin. Bobby Rowe was sitting in the desk chair. Mike Stemkowski and Frenchie Falcone were sitting on the built-in bench below the double portholes. They were dressed the way we used to dress when we were all hanging around the battalion command post with nothing much to do: faded green t-shirts, faded green utility caps, faded green jungle trousers, and jungle boots with all the polish scuffed off them.

"Jesus H. Christ!" I blurted out. "What the hell are you guys doing here?"

"We thought ya might like a little company," said Frenchie.

"But you're dead," I said.

"So what?" he said. "How do ya like my tattoo?" He pushed his short sleeve up and flexed his left bicep, on which was a tough-looking bulldog smoking a cigar and wearing a drill instructor's hat.

Bobby had been shot in the lung at Nui Loc San and had died a week later on a hospital ship. Ski had been hit in the head by shrapnel from a 152-millimeter artillery round at Con Thien; he had died on the medevac chopper. Frenchie had been shot dead instantly by a sniper in Hue City while riding shotgun in a jeep taking ammo and C-rations to what was left of Alpha Company.

"Got yourself a little problem, don't ya?" said Frenchie.

"Who told you that?"

"We hear things," said Ski.

"Word travels fast," I said.

"Don't it," said Frenchie.

"Yes, I've got myself a little problem."

"Smoke that demon weed, boy, gonna mess you up," said Bobby. His eyes twinkled.

5

"As if you guys are angels," I said.

"That's exactly what we are," said Frenchie.

"You think I'm a new guy or what? Where's your wings?"

"Jarheads don't get no wings," said Frenchie. "When did we ever get anything we needed?"

"How did you get here?"

"We walked," he said. "How the hell do we ever get anywhere? We ain't the First Air Cav, ya know."

"And thank God for that," said Ski. "The horse they can't ride, the line they won't cross, and the yellow for the streak down their backs."

"Never mind that," said Bobby. "What are we gonna do about you?"

"You didn't happen to bring a grenade launcher with you," I said. "Maybe some cyanide pills?" Frenchie laughed, a sort of choked little snort. "What's so funny?" I said.

"Come on, Slick," he said. "Don't ya get it?"

"Get what?"

"Ya kill people, beat 'em up, tie 'em up, lock 'em up, burn down their hooches, shoot their chickens an' their pigs an' their water bo, trash their crops, turn 'em inta shoeshine boys and shorttime girls, bop the little kids on the head with Ham and Motherfuckers, waste the forests, fuck up anything that moves or grows or stands more than six inches off the ground, an' they give ya a bunch a medals and a bunch a stripes an' a guaranteed VA home mortgage loan. 'Nice work. Fine work. You're a credit to the flag,' they say. Then ya smoke a little a God's contribution to peace, love, and happy days, and they wanna throw ya in the slammer. That's a laugh, don't ya think?"

"Frenchie, that's a regular laugh-riot. God forgive me, how could I have missed it?" Just then the door banged open and there stood Dutch. "Don't bother to knock," I said.

"All packed up," he said, looking around the cabin. Bobby, Frenchie, and Ski were gone. "Ja, dot's a gute boy." Dutch claimed to be Norwegian, but Roger and I were certain he was an ex-Nazi

U-boat commander wanted for crimes against humanity. He talked little and smiled even less. He didn't like anybody. "Bring your gear," he said. He had a smirk on his face, and his voice oozed something that must have been pleasure. I could see that face peering into the periscope, launching torpedoes, sending merchantmen to the bottom of the frigid North Atlantic, ramming the few lifeboats that had managed to get clear.

I picked up my seabag and followed him. We climbed the ladder to the boat deck, then stepped out onto the narrow catwalk suspended above the main deck between the afterhousing and the midship housing. It was a balmy March day in Long Beach, California, the sun very bright and well up in the sky. The great ship dwarfed the tiny figures scurrying over and around it. The relief crew worked down on the main deck, unhooking pipes and hoses from the manifolds, shifting booms, pulling hawsers, connecting other pipes and hoses, taking on refined oil for the next run north. It was a familiar rhythm of which I was suddenly no longer a part.

Dutch directed me bluntly to the radio officer's shack. Sparky was waiting for me. Ships' radio officers are always called Sparky. He had already prepared my discharge papers. "Sign here," he said, handing me a pen without looking up. "And here." He kept one copy and pushed the other across the table toward me. Only a few days before, Sparky and I had had dinner together in downtown Seattle with Roger the Engineer and the second mate. "Get off the ship," he said.

I stared at him for a moment. Then I looked up toward the ceiling, expecting to catch a glimpse of the bottom of a sixteen-ton weight just before it squashed me. It wasn't there. I picked up my seabag, threw it over my shoulder, and headed for the gangplank as fast as I could walk without looking like a kid who'd just plucked the cookie jar clean. Bloody hell, I thought, I'm outta here.

As I was leaving the midship housing, I passed Tom Collins, one of the able-bodied seamen and the ship's union shop steward. A pleasant, easy-going man, he had often stopped by my cabin just to shoot the breeze. A whiskey drinker by trade, he had come to appreciate marijuana enough to take a toke now and then. "They didn't even pay me," I told him, "They owe me two weeks' pay. And two months' vacation."

We didn't have a real union. What we had was a company union. A scab union. The real unions, the big maritime unions, had never been able to take over the company's ships because every time they negotiated a new contract with the other shippers, our company would offer its seamen just a little better deal. It cost the company something extra in the short run, but it was worth it. There were no strikes, no work stoppages, and no one willing to go to bat against management when a worker needed help.

"There's nothing I can do about it," Collins said.

"Thanks a lot," I said. As I cleared the gangplank, the four-to-eight oiler came walking down the dock toward the ship.

"I don't do this, mon," Winston said in his lilting Grand Cayman patois.

"Huh?" I said.

"Talk be in town, mon," Winston said. "Somebody say I tip them off, but I don't do that. Nevah do that. I swear it, mon. They search me, too."

"They fired me."

"I swear on my mother's grave."

"You seen Roger this morning?"

"He be at the Anchor and Spar. Go quick, you find him."

"You got cab fare? They didn't even pay me."

"You take this, mon," Winston said, pressing a $10 bill into my hand. "Okay, mon? You be okay?"

"Yeh, I'll be okay," I said. "Thanks, Winston." I found Roger where Winston said I would. He was hunched over a beer. He did a double take when he saw me. "They didn't arrest me," I said. "I don't know why. I didn't ask any questions."

"Want a beer?" said Roger.

"You buying?" I said.

8

"Yeh."

"They didn't get you?"

"No," he said, "They took my cabin apart, but I threw everything overboard before they got to me. Jake told me you put out the warning."

"And a lot of good it does me," I said.

"Your cabin was the first one they searched," said Roger, "They hit the port side lower passageway, then upper, then starboard. All the busts were on your passageway. Everybody else had a chance to clean up."

"Who else did they get?" I asked.

"John Cole, John Gavin, and Ramos. I heard they had to scrape seeds and stems out of Ray's carpet to bust him."

"What the hell, Roger?"

"Damned if I know," he said. "We got cocky and they got paranoid, I guess."

The drug of choice among sailors has always been alcohol. Drunks have been going to sea since Jonah fell overboard and claimed he'd been swallowed by a whale. The whole British fleet had been three sheets to the wind on navy grog at Trafalgar. I'd sailed with many a man who hadn't been sober since the Japanese attack on Pearl Harbor.

But by the early 1970s, a younger generation of sailors had taken the Age of Aquarius to sea. Smoking a joint on the stack deck in the early evening while watching a red ball sun set the Pacific Ocean on fire was a lot more appealing than guzzling whiskey. Even a few of the boozers, men like Tom Collins and Jake Smith, had gotten curious, putting the joint to their lips and sucking gingerly, as if they expected it to explode. But it never did, and we'd all gotten along just fine.

Only five days earlier, however, a company ship had exploded while unloading in Philadelphia. Several people had been killed and others had been seriously injured. The ship, though company owned, was flying a Panamanian flag and carrying a mongrel foreign crew. There were probably eight or ten languages on that

9

ship. God only knows what had actually gone wrong, but that didn't matter. It had been turned into a floating steel cinder.

"They had names," said Roger. "They went through the motions of searching everybody, but they knew who they were looking for. They opened up my toothpaste and took the top off my shaving cream, but they hardly touched Crosfield or Jensen. Somebody dropped a dime."

I told him what Winston had said to me.

"Not Winston," he said, "He's Rastafarian or whatever you call it. He wouldn't bring the heat down on his own religion."

"Maybe they had something on him," I said. "Maybe they blackmailed him."

"Not likely. I've known him a long time. He wouldn't do that."

"What about Scotty? He paid off the ship yesterday, and this morning the heat shows up."

"Scotty?" said Roger. "Gimme a break."

Until he'd left on vacation the day before, Panama Scotty had been the four-to-eight fireman for most of the time I'd been on the ship. He was in his mid-forties, lean and wiry with deep bronze skin and kinky hair going bald. He'd been in the Guatemalan navy until he deserted when the CIA had overthrown the Arbenz government in 1954.

"I didn't know Guatemala even had a navy," I'd told him one night as we'd stood gazing out of his porthole watching the stars fall into the sea.

"Oh, yes," he'd said, "A very nice navy. Little white boats that went putt-putt. So nice. Very nice. But the new government put guns on them, so I thought I had better leave. I don't like guns."

Scotty's cabin had been directly across the passageway from mine. He was always just coming off watch in the morning when I was coming on. I always knew, before I opened my door, that Scotty would be standing in his hatchway, moving rhythmically to the salsa music coming from his tape player, arms held out as if conducting the band.

"Ah, good morning to you, my friend," he would croon in his

smooth Caribbean English like cream being poured into a bowl of rose petals. "So nice to see you this morning. I was hoping you would pass my way. Have a little wake-up, my friend. It'll do you no harm." He would smile broadly as he extended one hand in my direction. Resting in his palm would be a Lucky Strike with one end emptied of tobacco and repacked with marijuana. I would take the cigarette and put it to my lips. Scotty would produce a match and, with just the hint of a flourish, light the end with the marijuana.

"Just a little wake-up, my friend," he would say. "It'll do you no harm. It's going to be a beautiful day today. Go and see for yourself. As for me, I am going to sleep. I love to sleep, don't you?" Then he would do a little samba, turn lightly as if floating, and close the door behind him. By the time I reached the maneuvering platform down in the heart of the engineroom, Scotty's little wake-up would be an ordinary cigarette.

"Okay," I said, "Not Scotty."

"My guess is one of the rummies got scared when the *Pathfinder* blew up," said Roger. "That was five days ago. Doesn't seem like a coincidence. We've never been raided before."

"What do I do now?" I said.

"At least you're not in jail," Roger said.

"Well, yes, there is that," I said, pulling out my Mastercharge card. "I don't know why they let me go, but I'm not going to stick around and see if they change their minds." We finished our beers and walked down the street to a car rental agency. I used the plastic to rent a car, and we drove to Los Angeles airport where I bought a ticket on the next plane to San Francisco, again using plastic.

"Why San Francisco?" he asked.

"I've got friends there," I said. "Hell, I don't know. I've got to go somewhere. They didn't exactly give me a whole hell of a lot of time to make plans. Sparky threw me off the ship without so much as a fare-thee-well. Wouldn't even look me in the eye. Collins wouldn't look at me either."

11

"They're all scared," said Roger. "Sparky and the rest of the rummies because they think you tried to blow them up. Everybody else because they know they just dodged a bullet. If they'd have done that raid right—clear out all the crew and then search the cabins—that ship would be as empty as *The Flying Dutchman* even as we speak."

"What about you?"

"I'm still shaking," he said. Roger had gone to the Massachusetts Maritime Academy. He was only a few years older than me, but he'd never been anything in his life except a seaman. He'd worked around ships and boats from the time he'd been old enough to walk. He'd gone to the maritime academy right out of high school. Sailing was all he knew. "I get fired for dope and I might as well go to jail because I'd never get another ship again."

"Where am I going to get another ship?"

"You don't need one."

"The hell I don't."

"You weren't going to stay out there anyway. We've had this conversation before. Who ever heard of a wiper with a college degree?"

"I was supposed to take my test for fireman next month," I said.

"Who ever heard of a fireman with a college degree? Okay, you were burned out. You needed a place to hang out for awhile. So you did that. Now go do something else. Why don't you write a book?"

"Jesus, you're no help."

Roger the Engineer was an electrical wizard and a patient teacher. Even when I was still a messman in the steward's department, he had carefully explained to me the workings of the massive turbines and the intricacies of the centrifugal water purifiers. He had taught me how to run the steam throttles and how to rewire the ship's ancient washing machine. He had helped to get me a transfer to the engineroom, where I could learn on the job instead of in my spare time.

More by chance than by design, the war in Vietnam had passed

Roger by. He'd had a draft deferment at the maritime academy, and his job as a licensed engineer aboard a U.S. merchant ship had also been draft-exempt. He had never met a Vietnam veteran before. "You weren't drafted?" he had asked.

"I wasn't even old enough to register for the draft," I'd told him.

"You volunteered? Why?"

When I'd first arrived in Vietnam, I had expected to be greeted by thankful peasants lining the roads, waving and cheering like the newsreels I'd seen as a kid of American GIs liberating French villages from the Nazis. The peace-loving people of South Vietnam were being invaded by cruel communists from the north. I was going to defend them. I was fighting for freedom. I was not going to ask what my country could do for me; I was going to do for my country.

What I found in Vietnam bore no resemblance to what I had been led to expect by Lyndon Johnson and *Time* magazine and my high school history teachers. The peasants of Vietnam had greeted me with an opaque silence that looked for all the world like indifference or hostility. And the cruel communists were indistinguishable from the people I thought I had been sent to Vietnam to defend. And the premier of South Vietnam was a French-trained pilot who wore tailored purple flight suits and admired Adolf Hitler.

At first appalled by the brutality and callousness of my brother Marines, in a few short months I found myself splitting an old man's foot to the bone with the flash suppressor of my M-16 because he would not or could not tell us where the mines and boobytraps were planted in his village, blowing up a family's house with dynamite because we'd found a hundred pounds of rice that might be used to feed the Viet Cong, throwing C-ration cans from a speeding truck at the heads of begging children just for laughs.

I had become something evil, but I did not know what it was or how it had happened or why. I didn't care. I just wanted to go home. And when that Freedom Bird finally lifted off the runway

13

out of Da Nang on the last day of February 1968, I thought I'd made it. I had survived, which had long since become the only purpose and the only victory imaginable. Whatever was going on in that sad and broken land, it wasn't my problem anymore. My war was over.

But the generals kept yakking, and the politicians kept yakking, and the bodies kept piling higher, and there was not enough whiskey in all the world to wash away the evil. In May 1970, when the Ohio National Guard opened fire on a crowd of students and protesters at Kent State University, killing four and wounding nine, I thought to myself, "It isn't enough to send us halfway around the world to die; now they are killing us in the streets of our own country." Then I joined the antiwar movement. Surely my country could not be as evil as it appeared. Surely the American people would listen to reason. I had served my country honorably. I had shed my blood for my people. Surely they would listen to me.

But they hadn't.

"I wish I'd gone to Canada while it still mattered," I had said to Roger. "Or Sweden. Lots of blondes in Sweden. But this'll do. Do you realize the whole Yom Kippur War was over before I even knew it had started?"

"What's that got to do with Sweden?" he had asked.

"That's why I'm here. No news, no cops, no hassles, three square meals a day, and I get to watch the porpoises. A man could do worse."

"You won't stay out here," he'd said.

"Watch me," I'd said.

"You've got a fire in your belly, boy. You've got a bee in your bonnet. You'll go back to the beach. You've got unfinished business."

"That's my flight," I said as the airport public address system crackled. "I better get going."

"I was right, wasn't I?" said Roger.

"About what?"

"I told you you'd go back."

"This wasn't my idea, pal."

"I never said whose idea it would be, did I?"

"Roger, something happened in my cabin this morning," I said.

"No shit," he said.

"I don't mean that," I said. "Something else. Something strange. There were these guys. I talked to three guys."

"What guys?"

"Guys I used to know. But they couldn't—Jesus, it was really strange. Oh, hell."

"What are you talking about?"

"Never mind. Forget it. Take the car back, will you?" I said, handing him the keys.

*   *   *

I spent the next several weeks with Mike Morris. The previous summer, 1973, I'd spent several months at his place, mostly sitting around watching John Mitchell and H.R. Haldeman and John Erlichman lie to the senate committee investigating the Watergate scandal and hoping that I would find a ship to take me away. Mike had driven me to the airport the morning the company had called to tell me I had a ship. It had been the first happy day I'd had since the grunts up on the amphibious tractors had started tossing live bodies down, bound hand and foot, and I had heard their cries and snapping bones and the first whisper that something was amiss.

"I've been floating around on a keg of oil with a bunch of drunks, and the assholes fire me because I blow a little dope," I said. "Frank Mulrooney used to wake me up at five-thirty in the morning looking for whiskey. He's supposed to be up on the flying bridge wing looking for icebergs and Russian trawlers and he's down in my cabin looking for whiskey."

"You're lucky you're not in jail," said Mike.

"Well, yes, there is that, but I don't feel lucky."

From San Francisco, I flew to Baltimore and holed up with my cousin. She lived in a big rowhouse with three or four other people, all of whom were fanatically devoted to Joni Mitchell. They made me listen to Joni Mitchell until the shrill warble of her voice, like the whine of a dentist's high-speed drill boring its way through enamel and bone, made me long for Vietnam or prison or any-place where I wouldn't have to listen to her ever again, so I took a bus to Charlottesville, Virginia.

There I stayed with a friend from college who was now in law school. He'd thought me a cool dude in college. Sergeant Rock. I had a car he could borrow any time he wanted to. I knew things other people didn't. I'd been in a war. Now I was in trouble, and I didn't have a car. Law school kept him very busy. He told me so himself. I left after two days.

I took a bus to Philadelphia and stayed with Daniel Kaufman and Sarah Faludi for awhile. No one had heard anything. No one had come knocking on doors in the middle of the night. No one seemed to be looking for me. Maybe it was safe to go home and see my parents. Still, I kept putting it off for as long as I thought I could get away with it. They were not going to be pleased.

Over the years, I had acquired some skill at not pleasing my parents. As a boy, more than once I had been asked to leave Sun-day School for misbehavior, no small embarrassment for the min-ister and the minister's wife, who happened to be my parents. When I was thirteen, I had argued with my father the night of Suzanne Steinway's birthday party. My father and I had already become something like strangers by then, and in anger he'd for-bidden me to go to the party, but I'd gone anyway, running out of the house barefoot and crying, walking to the party, wiping my eyes and nose on the inside of my shirt, making excuses to my friends about liking to go barefoot, even in March.

When I was sixteen, Pete Konrad and I had spent the summer in California. Pete had thrown a beer party one weekend in his parents' absence, but they'd come home a day earlier than they'd planned to, returning to a house in ruins, and it was not possible to say who was more surprised, his parents or Pete. The next day,

16

Pete had called me to say that he'd been grounded for the rest of the summer. "No way," he had said. "I'm going to California. Wanna come?" That sounded like a lot more fun than spending the rest of my summer as a lifeguard at Menlo pool, so we left the day after that, taking a train to Chicago, a Greyhound bus to L.A., and a municipal bus to Fullerton, where within three days we found both a $15-a-week room at the Allen Hotel and jobs in an aluminum sliding door factory called Silent Fold, Incorporated. It took our parents six weeks to figure out where we were. I got home the day before my senior year of high school started.

That November, 1965, on a Thursday night at ten o'clock, I took my father's yellow Volkswagen beetle and hit the road again, headed for the Homecoming Dance at Sunny Hills High School in Fullerton, where I imagined myself making a grand entrance to the amazement and delight of my California friends, but by Saturday morning I had run out of gas and money in Amarillo, Texas. Another twenty bucks and I'd have made it, but the Traveler's Aid folks in Amarillo wouldn't give me a dime until I called my parents, who had no idea where I was, and promised to drive straight back to Pennsylvania. I'd been too tired to argue, and anyway the dance was that night, and it was clear I wasn't going to get from Amarillo to Fullerton in time, no matter how fast I drove or how much money I had.

Four months later, I became the first student in the history of our school to get sent home from the senior class trip to Washington, D.C. I was caught smoking a cigarette in the men's room of Scholl's Cafeteria on the first day of the trip, and that night the school principal put me on a Trailways bus for home. Riding on that bus was a young Marine corporal in a dress blue uniform with orders for Vietnam. I'd already begun thinking about joining the Marines as early as the previous autumn, soon after the battle of the Ia Drang Valley, and the Marine looked so proud and confident in his uniform with its gold piping and red trouser stripes, and sounded so proud and confident when I asked him where he was going, that by the time I got off the bus, my mind was made up.

My parents did not want me to join the Marines. They had no political or moral objections, however; they just didn't want to see their son get killed when he could get a college education instead. Lots of kids from Perkasie joined the military, but not the kids the Pennridge school system deemed college material, the children of doctors and dentists and bankers and ministers. For all my extracurricular misadventures, I'd been an honor roll student, a member of the National Honor Society, and vice president of student council. My two older brothers were both in college already.

"Is this the way you raised me?" I'd finally asked after a long and circular discussion about my enlisting, "To let other mothers' sons fight America's wars?" It was not the way they'd raised me, and that had ended the discussion. I left for Parris Island the week after I graduated from high school.

I'd had a revelation in boot camp. I wanted my mother so badly, especially that first night, that I understood in a moment of blinding clarity what a saint she was and what a terrible son I'd been. I even realized that my father wasn't so bad either. Win some, lose some. He could have been worse. I wrote to them religiously, a letter a week from boot camp till just before I left Vietnam twenty-one months later. I never told them about the war. The night I got home, I hugged my father for the first time in as long as I could remember. It was the last time I would hug him for many years to come.

I didn't say much for a long time after I got back from the war, but I let my hair grow long, and wore beads and headbands and purple bell-bottom trousers. When I could feel again, for I had had to stop feeling in Vietnam because it was the only way to survive, what I felt was anger. Then I started to talk, mostly at very high decibels. By then, Lyndon Johnson was gone and Richard Nixon had invaded Cambodia, and the war I wanted to leave behind was stuck in my throat like a stick sharpened at both ends. I took a lot of it out on my parents because I was young and hurt and frightened.

18

My mother bore it all, year after year, with stoic patience. Her heart must have broken a thousand times, but she never let on. She loved her sons without qualification. She loved her husband, though it could only have been God's grace that gave her the strength to persist. When I was little, I couldn't understand why our house was so full of tension that you had to move through it as though you were swimming. By my early teens, I had stopped trying to understand, damning my parents equally and wishing to be free of both of them. Not until my twenties did I come to understand that the man my mother had married was not the man I knew. Much as wine will sometimes turn to vinegar, he had turned inward on himself as the years of their marriage had passed, and my mother had been left to hold her family together as best she could. As solid as a country church, she absorbed every sorrow, prayed for strength, and year after year somehow found it.

I never knew what ghosts haunted my father. Perhaps it was the loss of his father to the great flu epidemic of 1918 when my father was a newborn infant. Perhaps it was his doting mother, a practical nurse, working herself without mercy to support two small children. Or his older sister, who never forgave him for breaking up her happy trio of mother, daughter, and son by marrying that Eye-talian girl from town. Or the realization that he had sired four sons and did not know who they were. Maybe it was the loss of his dearest cousin during the Second World War. I knew that one bothered him.

Whatever it was, he burned slowly inward even as he showed a minister's face to the good people of Perkasie, lending a minister's ear to every troubled sheep, his reassuring smile beaming from the pulpit like a beacon. He was as fine a pastor as any congregation could want, and a son of a bitch to live with. It had taken me years to learn to like him, but I had learned because he was my father and you only get one.

Though I had not seen my parents in nearly a year, I was not looking forward to this visit. Of all the things I'd ever done that had not pleased them, this was going to take the proverbial cake.

19

All in one breath, I would have to tell them that I smoked marijuana and had just lost the sweetest job I was ever likely to find because of it. My mother had seen *Reefer Madness* when she was a teenager. A smalltown girl who had spent her summers at a Young Women's Christian Association camp, she had believed every word of it.

But it had been six weeks since they'd heard from me, and no doubt they were beginning to wonder if I had fallen overboard. Better to go see them before they called the company and started asking questions. So I got on a train and went home.

"Hi, Mom," I said, waving off her astonishment at seeing me walk in the front door. "Where's Dad?"

"He's over at the hospital," she said, "He's chaplain for the day. What are you doing here? Why haven't you written?" She was wearing her gardening clothes and had a pair of outdoor work gloves in her hand.

"Gardening?" I said brightly, kissing her on the cheek and putting my arms around her. "Want some help? What are you planting?"

She hugged me back hard for a moment, then pushed me away to arm's length, holding my waist in both hands. "Why are you home?" she asked. "Is something wrong?"

"I hadda come home for spring planting, didn't I? Let's get a move on here. Sun's darn near over the silo already." I took one of her hands and began to pull her toward the door.

"We don't have a silo," she said, shaking free, "and you haven't written for nearly two months. Now you show up unannounced. What's going on?"

"Come on, Mom, where's your sense of humor?"

"Enough," she said.

"Sit down, Mom," I said, "I've got to explain some things." As I talked, she sat there staring at me as if she were trying to take in Albert Einstein's general theory of relativity.

"But why?" she said when I had finished.

"It beats the hell out of getting drunk, Mom."

20

"I don't approve of that, either."

"When I get drunk, I get mean. But when I get stoned, I get mellow. Laid back and mellow, that's all. I've been smoking dope ever since Con Thien, Mom. Got a Good Conduct Medal and an honorable discharge. Got a college degree. It isn't like I smoke the stuff day and night, you know? I just like to get stoned once in awhile. You believe in God, don't you? Why would God invent the stuff if She didn't want us to smoke it? You don't have to re-fine it or distill it or anything. Just pick it and dry it and there you are. There's nothing wrong with it."

"It's against the law," she said.

"Well, yes, there is that. But who made it illegal? The guy who used to run the federal prohibition enforcement agency. He and his whole bureaucracy were about to be put out of work when prohibition was repealed, and they didn't want to end up on the street selling apples. Nobody but a few black musicians ever heard of marijuana till prohibition was about to be repealed. All of a sudden, it becomes America's number one threat. Evil enough to turn wholesome kids into murdering rapists. Guess who narrated *Reefer Madness*. The guy who used to be the head of the federal prohibition agency. Guess what happened to the federal prohibi-tion enforcement agency. It became the federal drug enforcement administration. Guess who became the boss. The guy who nar-rated *Reefer Madness*. This is true. Look it up. His name was Harry J. Anslinger. So marijuana is illegal, but it's okay to drop napalm on gooks. I should really pay close attention to what the dipsticks tell me is legal and illegal, don't you think?"

My mother had never gotten so much as a speeding ticket in all her life. Whatever the rules, whoever was in charge, she obeyed. It was not in her nature to question authority or challenge the received order of things. She had no idea what to do with what I was telling her. "But you've lost a good job," she said at last.

"Well, yes, there is that. Next time I'll be more careful."

My mother rolled her eyes toward heaven, as if she did not know where she or I had gone wrong. "Look, Mom," I said, "the world would be a better place if Richard Nixon got high once in awhile. You don't believe it, but that doesn't mean it isn't true."

"Oh, Bill," she said in voice so sad it almost startled me.

"Mom," I said. "You aren't going to change my mind, and I don't suppose I'm going to change yours, so what's the point in arguing? What's done is done. Let's do some gardening. Come on, I'll help you."

She never said another word about it. My father said even less, which was fine with me. It had all been easier than I'd expected, and I was glad to have it over with. I went back to Philadelphia and got a job in Havertown driving a forklift in a warehouse for minimum wage. Then I got a letter from the Coast Guard.

*   *   *

The letter arrived in an official envelope marked, "Penalty for Private Use $300." At the top of the page in bold letters on two lines was printed:

DEPARTMENT OF TRANSPORTATION
UNITED STATES COAST GUARD

The letter itself said, "Dear Sir: It is requested that you appear in person at this office at the first opportunity — Room 2042, Customhouse, 300 South Ferry Street, Terminal Island, California — for an interview with a Coast Guard Investigating Officer. Yours truly, Thomas J. Purcell, Lieutenant, Junior Grade, U.S. Coast Guard, Investigating Officer." Whoever had typed the letter and envelope had misspelled my last name. They were going to send me to prison, after all. For a moment I thought about Rio or Katmandu or Shanghai. Then I thought of George Martin.

During our senior year of college, George had gotten into a lot of trouble. A friend of his had been sending him cocaine in the mail from Colombia. Just a gram or two at a time, but enough to attract the attention of both the U.S. Post Office and the U.S. Customs Service. They'd shown up on campus one day, a whole

22

herd of narcs dressed like what they imagined hippie college kids dressed like. They stuck out like penguins in a tropical rain forest. Word of their arrival had reached George before they had. He'd managed to get rid of the coke, but they'd found a small stash of marijuana, and they were mad as hell that they'd screwed up, so they'd tried to throw the book at him. I remembered that George had been deliriously happy with his lawyer, and he had not gone to jail. I called him immediately and got the lawyer's name and phone number. I made an appointment for the following day.

When I walked into his office, Robert Richards stuck out his right hand and offered a smile that would have charmed the socks off my crusty old Connecticut Scots-Irish grandmother. He was a tall man, broad-shouldered, about forty-five, and his voice was clear and forceful. His hands were large and his handshake strong. "Now then, what can I do for you?" he said. "Do you want some coffee? Cream and sugar?"

"Just black," I said. "I drink my coffee black."

"Black coffee, Mildred, please," he called out the door. His office was in a converted house that was at least 200 years old. All the rooms were small, the doors and windows were small, and no two of them were the same size. The ceiling and floors slanted, the window glass was full of ripples and flaws, and the walls were thick. Richards dominated the room we were in.

"George Martin says you're a good lawyer," I told him.

"He ought to know," Richards said.

I handed him the letter I had received. He read it over, then looked across his desk at me. "Tell me about it," he said. If he weren't a lawyer, he might have been a priest, or a psychiatrist.

"I used to sail on tankers, too," he said when I'd finished. "With Gulf Oil out of Delaware City. We had those old Type Two tankers, leftovers from the Second World War. I still carry my merchant seaman's card. I've got it right here." He reached into his wallet and extracted a worn identification card with the photograph of a much younger man on it. "I sailed for two summers while I was in college. What are you going to do with the rest of your life?"

"Huh?" I said.

"What are you going to do with the rest of your life?"

"Let's see if I'm going to have one first, okay?"

"Okay, let me call this guy and see what's on his mind," he said, reaching for the telephone. He got through to Lieutenant Purcell on the first try. He explained who he was and then listened, occasionally offering comments: "Yes. Uh-huh. That won't be necessary. I'll have to request a change of venue. Yes, of course. I'll get that in writing to you right away. Okay. Thank you. Goodbye. You're going to be charged with misconduct," he said. "They want your seaman's card. If you give it to them, they'll drop the charges. If you don't, you'll have a hearing before a federal administrative law judge. We ought to be able to get that held in Philadelphia. What do you want to do?"

"I spent four years getting those papers," I said. "I was a good seaman. They owe me two weeks' regular pay and over two months' paid vacation time. I earned it."

"Actually, there's a good reason to fight this," he said. "If you turn over your papers, the Coast Guard will drop its charges. But the Justice Department might file criminal charges. This isn't a criminal proceeding. The Coast Guard only wants your papers. But possession of controlled substances in territorial waters is a federal offense, and you could still be liable under federal criminal law. On the other hand, the rules of evidence under administrative law are less stringent than under criminal law, so if the Coast Guard can't convict you in administrative court, the Feds won't bother to pursue it."

"And if they convict me in administrative court?" I said.

"Any subsequent criminal proceeding would still be under the stricter rules of evidence," he said, "so you'd be no worse off than if you turned your papers over without a hearing and then the Justice Department decided to file criminal charges. Of course, you could just hand over your papers and hope the whole thing blows over. It might."

24

"There's no way I'm going to hand over my card," I said.

"Do you think you'll ever sail again?"

"That's not the point."

"That's what I thought you'd say," he said.

"What would you do?" I said.

"It's not my papers they want," he said. "I just work for you."

"Then you'll defend me?"

"Of course," he said. "Everybody's entitled to a day in court."

"How can you do that?" I said. "How can you plead me not guilty when you know I am?"

"You haven't even been arraigned yet," he said. "How can you tell me you're guilty? Of what? Misconduct? What does that mean? Relieving yourself in public? Throwing spitballs? What have they got on you? They claim you've broken the rules. It's my job to find out if they've broken the rules. That's how I make my living. I'll call you when I have any news."

*　　　*　　　*

That spring of 1974, the Philadelphia Flyers won the Stanley Cup. I was still staying with Daniel and Sarah, living in a sleepingbag on the living-room floor of a second-floor apartment at 16th and Pine, and the day after the final game of the season, the city shut down and had a party.

I sat in the huge open bay window with my feet dangling out and nothing on but a pair of shorts, and watched all day long as people in cars streamed north on 16th Street and east on Pine Street, honking their horns and throwing anything portable out their windows: crumpled computer paper, shredded newspapers, tissues, pulverized styrofoam cups, whole pages from telephone books. Somebody tossed a bra. Socks and sneakers went flying. Baseball caps. Hockey pucks. It was a warm day in May, and the sun felt good. Everyone wanted to be happy.

The war in Vietnam was almost history. After ten years, it was no longer the lead story every night on the Six O'Clock News.

25

The bombs were still falling and the blood was still flying, but that was only a bad dream nobody wanted to think about. American boys weren't dying, and nobody cared what their tax dollars were doing. It was too disturbing. It was over.

Yet a nagging somewhere deep inside wouldn't go away. In Washington, D.C., Richard Milhous Nixon continued to twist slowly, slowly in the wind. He had fended off John Sirica, the presiding judge in the trial of the seven men who had broken into the Democratic National Headquarters in the Watergate complex, and Washington *Post* reporters Bob Woodward and Carl Bernstein, whose continuing investigation linked the White House to the burglary. He had weathered John Dean, his trusted young protégé who had decided to come clean about the whole Watergate affair, and bushy-browed Senator Sam Ervin, to whom Dean confessed during nationally televised hearings. But the noose was getting tighter.

From the beginning of his presidency, Nixon had ordered all Oval Office conversations secretly tape-recorded. He had not wanted posterity to miss a word. But the tapes had not remained a secret, and finally, after months of legal dodges and stonewalling, the White House had been forced to release the first transcripts of the tapes. Though incomplete and heavily edited—"expletive deleted" became a household phrase overnight—even in their sanitized form, they revealed that the man who had promised Peace With Honor was a mean-spirited emotional hunchback with the vocabulary of a peepshow operator and the morals of a shark. "I have never read such sleaziness in all my life," said House Minority Leader John Rhodes, an ardent admirer of Nixon's.

Millions of people hated Richard Nixon, but millions more believed in him and still wanted to: beat cops and bus drivers and secretaries, bank tellers and hardware store owners and the clerks who worked in the hardware stores, the Veterans of Foreign Wars, construction workers, volunteer firefighters and court stenographers. People who needed to believe that the long-haired, dope-smoking freaks were wrong. People who believed that Law and

Order were the first two amendments in the Bill of Rights. People whose own little lives could gain luster only if they were citizens of the greatest, freest, fairest, noblest, most powerful and congenial nation on earth.

The fire hoses and police dogs unleashed against Negroes singing hymns and offering prayers on a bridge in Birmingham, Alabama, had shown Americans something they had not wanted to see. Beefy police officers swinging their black polished nightsticks like so many Splendid Splinters in the streets of Chicago, their badge numbers taped to prevent identification, had shown Americans something they had not wanted to see. The bodies of men, women, and children strewn hugger-mugger in thick piles in a ditch at My Lai, gunned down by American boys like Jews in a Nazi concentration camp, had shown Americans something they had not wanted to see.

Richard Nixon had told them none of this was true. Richard Nixon had pledged to Bring Us Together. Richard Nixon, the hard-hat president, was going to hunker down and tough it out and show the malcontents and weaklings that America was still Number One. He had narrowly defeated Hubert Humphrey in 1968 on a promise to end the war in Vietnam. Four years later, though the war still raged, he had overwhelmingly crushed George McGovern to win re-election. Nobody cared about dead yellow people. Nixon had visited the Great Wall of China. Nixon had dined at the Kremlin. Nixon had given the pinkos and niggers what for at Kent State and Jackson, Mississippi.

But nobody slept well at night. What began as a second-rate bungled burglary had grown, in the words of bespectacled John Dean, like a cancer on the presidency. Even as the fires subsided in the urban ghettos and the antiwar movement went out with a whimper, the Watergate debacle grew and grew until there was not a day gone by without some new revelation.

The burglars had been working for the Committee to Re-Elect the President. They had also burglarized the office of the psychiatrist of Daniel Ellsberg, the man who had delivered the *Pen-*

tagon Papers to the light of day. The president had authorized hush money for the Watergate burglars. The president had ordered the Central Intelligence Agency to obstruct an investigation by the Federal Bureau of Investigation. The attorney general had blocked a major anti-trust action at the insistence of the president, who owed the Internal Revenue Service half a million dollars for cheating on his taxes. The national security advisor had ordered wiretaps on his own staff. The president's men, one after another, were being indicted and put on trial.

Through it all, the president continued to insist, "I am not a crook." But even to the dimmest of minds, the most hidebound of patriots, the notion that maybe the freaks had been right all along could not avoid insinuating itself. And that was too terrible to contemplate.

They didn't exactly turn on Nixon. They fell by the wayside in ones and twos, exhausted and confused. Richard Milhous Nixon had promised them that America was still Number One, and he had shown them a sewer. They didn't understand.

*   *   *

Richards and I went for an interview with the senior Coast Guard investigating officer at the U.S. Customs Building at Second and Chestnut Streets, an imposing structure towering over the Delaware River. From the 8th floor, I could see much of the river between the Walt Whitman and Benjamin Franklin Bridges, and the waterfronts of Philadelphia and Camden, New Jersey. There wasn't much traffic on the river, just a few pleasure boats and one tugboat chugging slowly north, pushing a barge, but eight or ten deepwater freighters stood at berths on both sides of the river. Soon they would cast off for Baton Rouge and Savannah and Galveston. Or maybe Copenhagen, Dakar, Brisbane, or Sao Paolo.

Richards and I were escorted into the office of Commander Maxwell Jeffries. Richards and Jeffries shook hands, then Jeffries extended his hand to me but withdrew it when I didn't offer mine.

Jeffries remarked upon the city's acquisition of the Stanley Cup. Richards responded that only Jesus saves more than Bernie Parent, the Flyers' goalie, and both men chuckled.

"So," said Jeffries, pausing to clear his throat, "I guess we might as well get down to business. Actually, we can clear this all up fairly quickly. Before we proceed, let me point out that this case is not against you per se. It's against your Merchant Mariner's Document. If you are willing to turn over your card at this time, you need only sign this affidavit attesting that you've relinquished your card voluntarily, and that's that. No further proceeding will be undertaken by the Coast Guard."

"Voluntarily?" I said.

"If you turn over your card," he said, "We can dispense with the matter right now."

"You gotta be joking," I said.

"Excuse me?" he said.

"I am not willing to turn over my card," I said. "It's mine."

Jeffries looked depressed. "I'm sorry you feel that way," he said. "The card is not yours. It was issued to you at the convenience of the United States Coast Guard."

"Then take it from me," I said.

"Very well," he said. "Here's a tentative draft of the charges that are to be preferred against you. I still have to consult with company officials before I can finalize this. You're entitled to representation by an attorney, a priest or minister, a company official, your union shop steward, a co-worker, friend, or anyone else of your choosing. One of our investigating officers will represent the government."

"What does the company have to do with this proceeding?" asked Richards.

"It's my understanding that the search was conducted by company officials," he said. "As you know, this matter was referred to us by our Long Beach station."

"There were no Coast Guard officers present during the search?" asked Richards.

"That's my understanding," said Jeffries. "As I said, this case was referred to us. I don't have all the details yet. I'll notify the judge and contact you when a hearing date has been set."

"You should have shaken his hand," Richards said to me when we were alone in the elevator.

"What for?" I said.

"It's polite."

"I don't like him."

"It's politic."

"I don't like politics."

"I didn't say politics," said Richards, "I said politic."

"Semantics."

"You want some coffee?" he said, steering me out the door of the customs building, across the street, and into a coffeeshop. "Let me explain something to you. The administration of the law, how laws are applied and interpreted, is highly subjective. I've known people busted with a lot more than you allegedly had who were never even charged. Cop decides the hell with it. For whatever reason, the men who busted you chose not to ignore it. Maybe you told them you thought they were joking."

"Oh, come on," I said.

"Who knows why? Maybe they didn't like breakfast that morning. Whatever. It doesn't matter. You didn't get over that hurdle, so now you've got to hire a lawyer and defend yourself. You go to your initial interview. Commander Jeffries has never met you before. He doesn't know you from Adam. He's only got a bunch of papers in front of him. If you make a good impression, he might decide you're a good-hearted lad who's made a youthful error. If you don't, he might decide that you're a rude, ill-mannered lout who deserves to be knocked down a peg or two. Which impression do you think you made on him today? Which kind of person is he likely to prosecute with more energy and conviction?"

"So I'm supposed to kiss the guy's ass," I said.

"Do you want to keep your papers or not?"

30

"I want to keep my dignity."

"There's nothing undignified about courtesy. You think it doesn't matter? Listen, once you get into a courtroom, anything can happen. God only knows how judges and juries reach their verdicts. You want to win? You learn to use every advantage. You asked me to help you. I need you to help yourself."

I knew that what he was saying was right, but it grated on me. Go along to get along. That's the way it worked.

Once, during the battle for Hue City, several of the scouts had found a woman willing to do the whole squad for a case of C-rations. Getting laid was not a high priority for me at that moment, and the idea of a gang-bang had seemed repugnant. But I'd gone along with it because I'd been afraid to say no. She hadn't seemed like a prostitute. She was only a girl.

Another time, during a firefight, Staff Sergeant Taggart had ordered me to fire on several old men whom we'd picked up earlier in the day and who had taken off running when the shooting had started. They had seemed more frightened and confused than intent upon escape, and I hadn't wanted to fire. But I had fired, killing one of them, the bullet entering the back of his skull and blowing the upper half of his face off.

What did such things have to do with what Richards was telling me? I wasn't sure, but something deep in my gut told me they had everything to do with each other. Dean Rusk, secretary of state under John Kennedy and Lyndon Johnson, who once claimed to have sensitive antennae, like a bug or a caterpillar, with which he could tell that the North Vietnamese were negotiating in bad faith, was a proper southern gentleman. Robert McNamara, secretary of defense under Kennedy and Johnson and a former president of General Motors, who thought he could beat a peasant army with flow charts and statistics, imagining human beings could be managed like oil filters and radiator caps, had been impeccably polite. Henry Kissinger, Nixon's national security advisor and later secretary of state, who considered the North Vietnamese "nothing but shits," had shaken hands with Le Duc Tho even as the B-52's were scouring eastern Cambodia. How many hands did I shake politely before I became like them?

*   *   *

That night I took a train to New York City to do a poetry reading with Jim Best, one of the editors of an anthology published by some vets from Vietnam Veterans Against the War that had included some of my poems. Jim had been to Vietnam in the days when Americans were still called advisors. He'd subsequently been appointed from the ranks to attend the U.S. Military Academy, but the memory of a Buddhist nun burning herself to death on a street in Ninh Hoa had followed him all the way to West Point, New York. She had doused herself with gasoline, calmly struck a match, and turned herself into fire. She had sat there motionless and silent until nothing remained but a husk. His instructors had told the new cadets that in four years they would be leading combat platoons in Vietnam. "Not me," he had said, and he'd resigned his appointment.

We were reading in the basement of a Catholic church on West 47th Street between 9th and 10th Avenues. The audience was small, a handful of friends and antiwar diehards who had seen too much to become insurance salesmen and didn't have the money to go to Jamaica. When we finished, most of us decided to adjourn to a tavern over on 8th Avenue for a few beers. Jim and I had some boxes of books we didn't feel like lugging around New York, so we sent the others on and headed over to 10th Avenue to put the books in Jim's car.

As we came around the corner onto 10th, several police cars, their lights flashing, clustered together at the far end of the block. They must have been there for awhile because we hadn't heard any sirens. We stashed the books, then we headed back up 10th and turned the corner onto 47th. We'd gotten halfway back down the block, almost directly in front of the church, when I heard footsteps running in the street behind me. Just as the thought was registering that someone was approaching in a hurry, I heard, "Freeze! FREEZE!!"

I turned to look and found myself staring into the muzzle of a pistol. It had a very large bore. I could have stuck my head in it. The man who held it was dressed in street clothes and was down in a crouch with the pistol in both hands, arms fully extended. "Up against the wall!" he shouted. "Now! Move!"

"What the hell do you think you're doing?" Jim started to say, but I had already grabbed him by the upper arm and was spinning him with me.

"That's a gun," I said. I put my hands on the wall above my head, spread wide, and leaned into the wall.

"You know the position, don't you?" the man said, kicking my feet farther apart. "I got two on 47th between 9th and 10th," I could hear him say into a hand-held radio.

"What the hell is this?" said Jim. "You've got no right to arrest us."

"Just stand there," said the cop.

"We've been right across the street all night," Jim said. "In that church. We were doing a poetry reading, for chrissake!"

"Right," said the cop. "So's my mother."

A moment later, a mob of cop cars came roaring down the street from both directions, lights blazing, sirens going like gangbusters. Suddenly cops were everywhere. "New York City police!" one man barked, waving something shiny in front of my face while someone I couldn't see patted me down, then snapped a handcuff on my right wrist, twisted my right arm behind my back, whipped my left arm back and cuffed it to the right one, then started pulling me toward a cop car.

What the fuck, I thought, and this time they've got guns. It couldn't be dope. I was clean. Jim was clean. Bust us for a lousy poetry reading? Maybe plant something on us? They could slip a baggie into a pocket, a little grass or coke or heroin. Then things would get interesting.

They pushed us both into the back seat, one from either side. Jim and I looked at each other. I wanted to check my pockets, but my hands were cuffed behind my back. "There's the priest, for chrissake," Jim said. Not twenty yards away, the priest who'd offered us his church was stepping out the door. "Ask him. Ask him. He'll tell you who we are." The priest locked the door behind him, then turned and walked in the opposite direction. The street was full of cop cars and cops, but the priest didn't even look our way. Just another night in America. The cops watched him go.

They drove us to the Midtown North Manhattan Precinct station. With a cop on either arm, we were hustled out of the car, through the building, and into a bare room where we were manacled to chairs. They went through our wallets and asked us a bunch of questions.

"My wife's waiting for us at Nelson's," Jim said. "At least call her and tell her where we are."

"We're supposed to get one phone call," I said.

"We haven't arrested you yet," said a cop.

"Right," I said, rattling the handcuffs against the chair.

"You don't get a phone call until we book you," the cop said. Then they went away.

Four hours later, they released us. A liquor store on 10th Avenue had been robbed at gunpoint. The store owner had said that two of the robbers had run up 10th Avenue and turned east on 47th Street. We had been the only two people the plainclothes cop had seen.

"So we must be the guys," Jim said.

"Sorry," said one of the cops.

"Meanwhile, the real crooks are halfway to Minnesota," I said.

"You're free to go," said another cop.

"His wife's waiting for us twenty blocks from here," I said. "It's two o'clock in the morning. We don't get a ride or anything? A subway token?"

"We're busy," one of the cops said.

* * *

A few days after my non-arrest for armed robbery, Sarah told me the landlady had complained to her about me sitting naked in the bay window above 16th Street. I liked to sit in the window and watch the street, even when there wasn't a Flyers party. It was like watching a movie about life.

All sorts of things went on. Fender-bender accidents and ambulances running red lights. Couples holding hands, or kissing, or shouting at each other. One day I'd seen a man dragging a bathtub down the street. Another day, two women got into a fistfight over a parking space. They were throwing haymakers at each other. A John Lennon look-alike tried to throw a joint up to me one time, but he couldn't make it reach the second floor. A bag lady picked up a beat-up hat from the gutter, tried it on, grimaced, and walked away quacking like a duck.

There was an ice cream store just around the corner on Pine Street. I couldn't see the store, but I got to see happy customers all the time. Some of them weren't so happy. One little boy licked the ice cream right out of its cone. It plopped onto his shoe. He stood there staring at the empty cone in his hand, as if Merlin the Magician had made the ice cream disappear. Then he looked down at his shoe and began to cry. His mother started to yell at him, then thought better of it and curled him into her arms.

I liked to call greetings down from my perch. "Nice day, isn't it? How are you today?" Things like that. Sometimes people would look up and wave and say hello. Sometimes they'd look up and blink and turn back into themselves. If they did that, I would try to guess their names. "You must be Edward," I would call down. "Victoria? I'll bet your friends call you Vicky." They would scuttle away like crabs. Sometimes I would sit there for hours without saying anything, the way I used to sit up on the stack deck of the ship or out on the berm at the battalion command post north of Hoi An.

"I don't sit there naked," I said to Sarah.

"Well, that's the word she used."

"It's illegal to take your shirt and shoes off in the summertime?"

"She's an old lady," Sarah said. "Why don't you just put a shirt on?"

"What for?" I said.

"Why does everything have to be a fight with you?"

"Did I start this? I'm just sitting in the window watching the world go by. Why can't people mind their own business?"

"She owns the building," Sarah said, "I've got to deal with her. You don't. Wear a shirt or stay out of the window. This isn't your apartment." Then she stalked into the kitchen.

Sarah had been a year behind me in college. I'd had a date with her once, but she'd broken it to go motorscooter riding with some dork whom even Sarah admitted, some years later and with some embarrassment, had been a dork. Eventually she'd started dating Daniel, and when he'd graduated, she had dropped out of college and moved in with him, getting a job in the personnel department of the Philadelphia Art Museum. I earned my keep around the apartment by washing dishes. She wouldn't let Daniel do the dishes because he was always in too much of a hurry and left soap all over everything, but I was a very careful dishwasher.

What drew me to their apartment was Daniel. A year ahead of me in college, he had been a serendipitous friend at a time when I was just discovering that I had fought for a two-bit puppet state in South Vietnam invented and perpetuated entirely by the muscle and money of the U.S. government. If he took anything seriously, I had yet to discover what it might be. He seemed to move through life impervious to its outrageous slings and arrows, finding grand humor and entertainment in the ambitions and the foibles of the high and the lowly alike. During my years in college, when I'd been the only Vietnam veteran in the midst of a sheltered and privileged student body that had never allowed me to forget how different I was, Daniel had been a saving grace, caring not one whit whether I had been to Vietnam or Mars or Borneo.

For most of my first year in college, I had dated a young woman who had fallen in love with the romance of an ex-Marine sergeant who wrote poetry. But she had found herself, like the United States in Vietnam, riding the back of a tiger. The day after Nixon invaded Cambodia and the day before the shootings at Kent State, I'd been up in Pam's room trying to study when she'd returned from an antiwar meeting at the student center. I was still trying to believe that my war was over. She'd asked me if I'd like to go to the next day's meeting.

"What the fuck do a bunch of college kids know about anything?" I had shouted with a vehemence that had startled both of us, kicking a tin pretzel can sitting on the floor next to the desk, which sent the contents flying all over the room. Pam had laughed at that, and I had turned on her as quickly as I had once fired into the darkness at the sound of a snapping twig, throwing a punch with all my might that struck her flush on the shoulder and sent her flying onto the bed.

It was the first and last time I ever struck a woman, but the damage had been done and the relationship, already on shaky ground because of my volatile temper and unpredictable mood swings, petered out over the next few months. Still, when school began again the following September, we couldn't quite stay away from each other, she because I had been her first real lover and she liked it, I because I wanted the warmth of a woman to stave off the cold that had locked onto my soul in the ricefields and hamlets of Vietnam and would not let go. She would go home on weekends to visit her old high school boyfriend, then return Sunday nights and sleep with me. It was better than nothing, or seemed so at the time.

But after a few months, she began to date another student at college, and it was too much for me to see them walking together across campus or sitting together in the dining hall. One night I went to his room to beg her to leave him. I knew she was there, but he wouldn't let me in, so I hit him in the throat. The blow dropped him immediately. He lay on the floor gasping and choking, unable to draw breath while I stood over him crying and shouting obscenities. I drew back my foot to kick him in the face.

And then I stopped, my foot still suspended in the air. My father had taught me how to be angry, but the war had taught me how to vent that anger through the exercise of brute force. No more, I thought. No more. I turned away and walked back to my room, and by dawn I had drunk a quart and a half of whiskey. I did not leave my room for three days. Daniel never asked what happened and I didn't tell him, but twice a day he would knock on my door to make sure I was still alive, bringing food from the dining hall and leaving it on the floor just outside the door.

So after the bust, when I needed a place to stay, I'd turned to Daniel. It was not a large apartment, and Sarah and Daniel hadn't had too much privacy since I'd arrived. As I listened to Sarah banging pots and pans around in the kitchen in a manner that suggested irritation, it occurred to me that I had overstayed my welcome. I started looking for a new place to live.

I found one in Swarthmore, eleven miles west of Philadelphia. Someone offered me the attic of a small house. I could stay there until October. The attic was unfurnished except for a bed, a desk, and a chair, and there were no big windows and no street people to watch, but it came rent-free and was close to the train station and bus stop. I moved in immediately.

*   *   *

Every few weeks, I would take the train home to see my parents. I never saw anyone else while I was home, but sometimes at night I would borrow my father's car and drive to the park where Jeff Alison, Max Harris, and I used to play war. We were brave soldiers, the three of us, reckless with our lives, storming the old chicken coop in the woods to rescue Ursula Netcher, Cathy Wolfinger, and Carol Weidemoyer from the Germans. Or I'd drive up to the ridge and park in the cemetery, from where I could see the whole shallow valley in which the town nestled as if Norman Rockwell had put it there with brushes and paint.

It was a small town surrounded by small family farms. There'd been no traffic lights when I was a kid, and only one fulltime cop. Nothing much ever happened. In the summer, we would ride our bikes to the Kellys' farm and chase the cows, squirting pink-eye lotion into their eyes until they would get mad and chase us instead, and in the winter we could walk to the creek and go ice skating. We'd bob for apples at Halloween and go from front porch to front porch caroling at Christmas. Every Memorial Day we'd decorate our bicycles with red-white-and-blue crepe paper and join the big parade down Market Street that always ended at the little war memorial where the American Legion color guard would fire a salute to the dead in battle who had made it possible for us to have this good and gentle town.

I was taught that freedom does not come cheaply, and I learned there were those who wished to take that freedom away from me. In elementary school, I had cowered under my desk with my head between my knees and my hands clasped behind my neck, practicing what to do if the Russians ever dropped an atomic bomb on us. When I was fifteen, my oldest brother and I had driven to Washington and stood in line for eight hours one cold November night just to get a glimpse of John Kennedy's closed casket. When I was sixteen, I had ridden around town on the back of a flatbed truck singing Barry Goldwater campaign songs because Goldwater had said, "Extremism in defense of liberty is no vice." And in the autumn of 1965, when American soldiers in the Ia Drang Valley tangled for the first time not with Viet Cong guerrillas but with North Vietnamese regular army troops, I knew my duty.

I'd gotten my picture in the local weekly newspaper when I enlisted in the spring of 1966, and most of my high school teachers, one after another, had stopped me in the halls to shake my hand and offer me their congratulations. They were as sure as I was, for they had taught me, that anyone willing to challenge the United States of America must be up to no good, and though they didn't say it to my face, they were equally sure that Marine Corps discipline was just what was needed to tame the rebellious streak in the preacher's errant son. They even chose me as one of the three student commencement speakers.

When I came back from Vietnam nearly two years later, I discovered that my best friend, Jeff Alison, who had flunked two grades and was two years behind me in school, had just left that day for his senior class trip to Washington, so I'd decided to drive down early the next morning to see him. I'd found him having breakfast in the restaurant of the Chevy Chase Motor Lodge. The chaperons were all sitting at one table. They had known me all my life. They went to my father's church, and played golf with him, or baked pies with my mother for the town's swimming team bake sale.

But on that morning, not one of those teachers said a word to me. They just stared at me as if they were seeing a ghost. I waved cheerily, but they didn't even blink.

"What's their problem?" I said to Jeff as I sat down.

"Beats me," said Jeff. "Have some toast."

I was well into a western omelet when Mr. Ettison, the school guidance counsellor, got up and came over. He was a deacon in my father's church.

"Hi, Mr. Ettison," I said, "Bet you didn't expect to see me here."

"Hello," he replied gravely. "What are you doing here?"

"Well, I was in the neighborhood," I said, grinning broadly. He didn't smile back. "No, actually, I came to see Jeff. I just got back from Vietnam, you know? I haven't seen him in more than a year. I wanted to see Jeff, that's all."

"I think you'd better leave," he said. "We don't want any trouble."

"I'm not going to give you any trouble, Mr. Ettison. I just—"

"Good," Ettison said, "I appreciate that. Why don't you just finish up here and go?"

"Hey, what's the matter with you? What did I do? I haven't done anything wrong."

"We've got three hundred students here, and we don't want any trouble—"

40

"I can't eat breakfast in a public restaurant with my best friend?"

"—I've already told the management if they rent you a room, we'll cancel the school's contract with them—"

"I'm not staying!" I said. "I just—"

"—if I see you anywhere in the motel, I'll call the police."

"Call the police?!" I said. "What's your problem, man? What, I go to Vietnam, do my duty, suddenly I'm a criminal or something?!"

"I won't argue about this," Ettison said, his bald head glistening with perspiration.

"Hey, you ain't my teacher anymore," I said, "I don't have to take this kind of crap from you."

But I did have to take it. What was I supposed to do? Wait around till he called the cops? Punch him out? "That bald guy's paying," I said to the waitress as I got up to leave. "Him right there. You," I said, pointing at Ettison.

Whether the chaperons' concerns were generic or specific to me, connected in some way to my having been in Vietnam, or the continuing consequence of late night runs to Amarillo and cigarettes in the men's room of Scholl's Cafeteria, Mr. Ettison never bothered to explain, but it was painfully obvious that my elders had been far more eager to send me off to war than to welcome me home from it. I had been back from Vietnam less than a week, but already it was becoming difficult to think of Perkasie as a place where I belonged.

A few years later, in the spring of 1971, I stopped by the Mayflower Bar to pick up a six-pack of beer to take back to college. The bartender wouldn't sell it to me, and he and several of the customers began to make fun of my long hair, calling me a faggot and a pussy. For a moment I had considered taking on the whole place, but this was after Kent State and Jackson State, and Perkasie had two traffic lights by then, and it occurred to me that Chief Nellis might actually shoot. These were the people I'd gone to Vietnam for, I thought, looking around the bar. "You weren't worth it," I said.

I had already stopped talking to most people in town by then; I had little to say to them, and nothing they wanted to hear. After the incident in the Mayflower, I would not buy anything in Perkasie. Not beer or gas or even a magazine. Max was dead. He had served two years as a Marine in Vietnam only to die one night while riding his motorcycle through town at high speed with no headlight or helmet. Jeff, whom the Pennridge school system had written off as a dummy by the time he was ten years old, had moved to Florida, having avoided both the draft and the war by what wisdom or luck I had no idea, though I'd always known he was smarter than anyone thought.

So when I went home to see my parents, that's exactly what I did. On one visit, I took down the old dead apple tree in the backyard, smoothed off the stump, and built a flowerbox on top of it. Then I dug up the soil around the base of the tree, and bordered the whole thing with a ring of stones I dragged out of the vacant lot behind our yard. My mother planted flowers.

*   *   *

That night I drove up to the cemetery and parked. It was a warm spring night and the lights of the town, in the clear still air, seemed like carillon bells. I could see soldiers burning the homes of the people of Perkasie, raping their daughters and wives, shooting their husbands and sons, their mothers and their dogs, churning their tree-lined streets to rubble, but the people of Perkasie could not and would not see it. I got out of the car and found Max's grave in the darkness.

"Somebody ya know?" said a voice. I jumped involuntarily.

"Jesus Christ, Frenchie, don't do that." Frenchie, Bobby, and Ski were back.

"Sorry 'bout that," said Frenchie.

"Quit sneaking up on me," I said. "Goddamn, can't you telephone first, or knock or something? You guys are supposed to be dead."

"We are dead," he said.

"You don't look like you've aged a day," I said.

"We haven't," said Bobby. "You don't sound very happy to see us."

"That was you guys on the ship, wasn't it?"

"Who'd ya think it was?" said Frenchie. "The Three Stooges?"

"Have you any idea how weird this is?" I said.

"I know what you mean," said Ski.

"How do you think we feel?" said Bobby.

"So they ain't sent ya to prison yet," said Frenchie.

"Not yet, but they're working on it. What are you two doing with Bobby? He got killed six months before either of you showed up. You never even met."

"We met later," said Bobby. "We're all in the same outfit now. When you get killed, you get sent to Battalion Rear. I was there when Ski and Frenchie showed up. Been together ever since. Everybody's there. Everybody who got greased. Aymes, Thurston, Roddenbery and Maloney, Basinski, Scanlon. They're all there."

"You mean when I die, I've got to spend the rest of eternity in the Crotch?"

"Sorry, not you," said Bobby. "You made it back to the World. You have to be Missing In America for the rest of your life. Then you can go home."

"Don't you guys get to go home?"

"When the war's over," said Ski. "I used to think I'd get home before you, but now I'm not so sure."

"I tried, guys," I said. "I joined VVAW. I tried to talk to people, but nobody would listen."

"We know," said Ski.

"I even put on a coat and tie and went to the Rotary Club. Rotary Club, for chrissake. I laid it all out for 'em. I told 'em about search and destroy missions, harassment and interdiction fire, winning hearts and minds. All that stuff. What it sounded like on paper and what it came down to out in the villes. Was I ever sharp that day. If I'd been a salesman, I coulda sold the Brooklyn Bridge."

"Don't get smart," said Frenchie. He was an Italian kid from

Brooklyn. He had a sentimental attachment to the Brooklyn Bridge.

"No, no, listen," I said, "You won't believe this. I got done and nobody said a word. No applause. No nothing. Then this skinny old fart shaped like a cold chisel gets up and says he's a retired bird colonel, and he thinks we should keep pounding those little yellow bastards until they do what we say or we kill 'em all, and he tells me I can't be a real veteran because a real veteran wouldn't go around badmouthing the good old U.S. of A., and the whole place erupts in thunderous applause."

"We can believe it," said Ski. "There's guys in Battalion Rear still talking like that. Missing a sparkplug or two. We don't pay any attention to 'em. They're as dead as we are, the dumb fucks."

"I didn't want you to think I just skyed out and left you there," I said.

"We don't think that," said Frenchie.

"It's our parents' fault," said Bobby. "They let us go. They bought the whole stupid spiel: hook, line, and sinker. They coulda asked a few questions. They coulda said no."

"We bought it, too," I said. "Who was gonna tell us anything? Would you have listened to 'em? If my parents wouldn't have signed the papers, I'd have waited three months and enlisted on my eighteenth birthday, that's all."

"I don't mean us," said Bobby. "They coulda said no to the government. They coulda stood up to those jackasses in Washington. They coulda said, 'You can't have our kids. Send your own kids. Go fight 'em yourselves.' But they didn't."

"Now they gotta believe it meant something," said Frenchie.

"Kinda disappointing to find out your parents aren't what you always thought they were," said Ski.

"Nothing's the way we thought it was," I said.

"I know what you mean," he said.

"Who's in that grave?" said Frenchie. "Somebody ya know?"

"Yes," I said. "A dead Marine. Ex-Marine, actually. Kid I grew up with. His name's Max Harris. You seen him around?"

"No, he's not with us," said Ski. "You had to get killed in country to get sent to Battalion Rear. What'd he die of?"

"Government lunacy," I said.

"That's funny, Slick," said Frenchie, "Whaddaya mean?"

"Folks down there think he got killed in a motorcycle wreck," I said, gesturing toward the lights below, "but he was a dead man long before that. After his first tour ended, he extended for six months. Then he extended again. They wouldn't let him extend the third time he put in for it."

"Don't take it personal," said Ski, "But somebody extends three times, he's gotta have a few screws loose."

"I don't think so," I said. "I bumped into him on Okinawa, at Camp Hansen. I was just going over and he was going back on his first extension. He told me he didn't think anything going on in Vietnam was worth the life of a single Marine. When I asked him why he was going back, he said, 'Cause there ain't much worth staying home for.'"

"Are you kiddin' me?" said Frenchie. "Nice little town like this?"

"It's not what it looks like," I said, "I didn't know what he meant back then, but I do now."

"Reminds me of the town I come from," said Bobby. "Only it's a lot flatter in Nebraska."

"Folks there think God wears an Uncle Sam suit?" I asked.

"Yep," said Bobby.

"You know what I'm talking about, don't you?" I said.

"Yep," said Bobby.

"I'd rather be here then dead," said Frenchie.

"If Max isn't with you guys," I said, "Where is he?"

"How should we know?" said Frenchie. "I guess they sent him to the regular dead place."

"He ought to be with you," I said. "They killed him just as sure as they killed you."

"Well, he ain't," said Frenchie, "And that's that."

"Listen up," said Ski, "We didn't come here just to shoot the shit. We need a favor."

"What is it?"

"We need Nixon's phone number."

"What?"

"You still deaf?" said Frenchie. A few days before Frenchie had gotten killed, I'd been splattered with shrapnel from a B-40 rocket. My body armor had absorbed much of the impact, but the blast had left me stone-deaf for weeks.

"What the hell do you need Nixon's phone number for?" I said.

"We're gonna tell 'im to get off your case," said Bobby. "We don't like him fuckin' with you this way."

"We're gonna tell 'im he oughta smoke a little smoke hisself," said Frenchie. "Take 'is mind off things. Lighten up a bit."

"I can handle it," I said. "I've got a good lawyer."

"Hey, anything can happen in a courtroom," said Ski. "We're just gonna lean on him a little."

"Well, that's damn thoughtful of you, guys, but I don't know his phone number."

"Get on your case for smokin' a little smoke," said Frenchie. "Look what they done to us. And then they make a big deal outta smokin' a little smoke."

"Don't you get it, Frenchie?" I said. "You told me it's supposed to be funny."

"Come on," he said, "Get a phone book. We'll jus' blow a little smoke up 'is backside."

"It wouldn't do any good, Frenchie. There's a million more just like him. Besides, where am I supposed to get a Washington phone book in the middle of the night? He's probably not even listed. Anyway, like I said, I got a good lawyer. I'm doing okay so far. Maybe you could just keep an eye on things. Maybe if things don't go right."

"Yeh, okay," said Ski. "We'll cover your flanks for you. But you watch your step, okay?"

"Okay," I said. "Thanks, guys."

"Once a Marine, always a Marine," said Frenchie.

"Don't say that," said Bobby.

"Sit down for awhile," I said. We'd all been standing. "The grass is a little wet, but what the hell."

We all sat down in front of Max's headstone, all four of us close together like we used to huddle around someone's cot in the hooch late at night when we were back in the battalion CP and somebody'd gotten a hot love letter and he'd read it to us by flashlight, pressing the light against the paper so only a dim glow shone around the edges of the rim. Somewhere across town, a dog started barking. Then half a dozen more dogs joined in.

"What's it like?" I said.

"It's not so bad," said Bobby. "Mostly we do the same shit we always did. Fill sandbags. Play cards. Hang around. Hump the boonies once in awhile, 'cept nobody ever gets killed because we're all dead already. Sometimes we go over and chow down with Charlie. They're all dead, too, so they don't care. We swap war stories, show each other pictures, talk about what we were gonna do when we got home. There's this one little guy, got killed in a B-52 strike up along the DMZ, he's got a wife that's the goddamnedest knockout I ever laid eyes on. Cute as a button. And two little kids, boy and a girl. Every time we go over there, he shows me that picture. They don't even know he's dead yet. Just headed off down Uncle Ho's trail one day, and that's the last they heard of 'im. They got thousands of guys like that. And women, too. Can you imagine?"

"Makes me laugh when I hear people whining about them not giving our guys back," said Ski. "Our guys are dead, too."

"You seen any of 'em?" I said.

"Oh, sure. We told ya, everybody's there. Everybody that got killed there. They ain't in our outfit, though. Most of 'em are flyboys, officer-types, but we see 'em around."

"We got Kenny's arm," said Frenchie. "It showed up the day you and Kenny got hit. We got it hangin' up in the hooch right next to Pelinski's shorttime calendar. Looks kinda classy."

"Nobody else has one," said Ski.

"What about you?" said Bobby. "You doing okay?"

"I guess so," I said.

"Kinda lonely, aren't you?" he said.

"Yeh."

"I know what you mean," said Ski.

"Don't ya hear from any of the guys?" Frenchie said. "Rolly or Wally or Mogerdy? Sergeant Seagrave?"

"I saw Gerry once," I said. "A few years ago when I was driving around. I went up to Oregon and looked him up. His knee's healed up pretty good. We went trout fishing and we had a nice time, but it was kind of sad, you know? Things change. He's got a family now. Two little boys. Goes to church and all. I tried to get him to join VVAW, but he said he'd lose his job if he did. And his wife didn't like me. There's this big hole in Gerry's life, and she doesn't understand it and she knows I do. That scared her. I haven't tried to find anybody else since then."

"Some ways, we're better off where we are, I guess," said Bobby.

"I know what you mean," said Ski.

"That's you guys' opinion," said Frenchie.

"Hey," I said, "I have fun sometimes."

"Sure you do," said Bobby.

"No, really. I'm getting along okay."

"We gotta get along, too," said Frenchie. "We got an LP at oh-two-hundred. Gonna set up on the far side of that ville at the northwest corner of the berm."

"Can't you stay awhile longer?"

"Gunny Johnson's sergeant of the guard tonight," said Ski. "He'll have the ass if we ain't ready in time. He still makes us do the greasepaint and all that John Wayne stuff."

"We'll come back," said Bobby. "Why don't you go home and get some sleep now?"

"I will," I said. "Soon."

"And don't worry," said Ski. "We'll be watchin' your flanks."

Bobby reached out and touched my cheek with his fingertips. His eyes met mine and held them for a moment. Then the three of them stood up and walked into the darkness, strung out single file at five-meter intervals, as if they were on patrol. I could see the headlights of a car out on Branch Road about a mile east of town. It turned right onto Blooming Glen Road, climbed up the long shallow grade toward the Mennonite church, then disappeared behind some trees.

I spent all of the next morning fixing up my younger brother's abandoned three-speed bicycle and took it back to Swarthmore. I would rather have had a car, but the bike got me around town faster than walking.

*   *   *

I could even ride to Robert Richards's office, which was only four miles away. A hearing date had been set, and we had begun to prepare. When I complained about the slowness with which the Coast Guard was proceeding, Richards had said, "Delay is always to the advantage of the defense."

"Why?"

"Memories fade. Recall becomes more difficult. The chain of custody gets longer. More chances for mistakes. Don't be in such a hurry," he said. "Patience is a virtue. I've been doing some research, and I think we're in a pretty good position. They've never had a case like yours. Mostly what they get are seamen who get busted ashore by police and tried in criminal court. Then the Coast Guard simply submits the record of the criminal proceeding as evidence. The fact of the misconduct is already established by the criminal conviction. Do you remember our meeting with Commander Jeffries? He said you had the right to an attorney—or a priest or a minister, or Manny, Moe, and Jack, or the Tooth Fairy. They aren't accustomed to handling these hearings like real trials. Usually the defense consists of some union shop steward who tells the judge what a swell guy Joe Blow is. Then the judge lifts Joe Blow's ticket and the case is over. With you, they've got to prove at least one of the specifications before they can prove misconduct. I don't think they've had a lot of experience doing that, and that works to our advantage."

"So you think we've got a chance?"

"Of course I think we've got a chance. I always think I'm going to win. Anything can happen once you get into a courtroom, but I like our position better than I did when we started."

"How did you find out all this stuff?" I asked.

"It's my job," he said. "Look at this." He held up one of two large leatherbound books titled *The Law of Seamen*. "One of my clients is a retired chief engineer. I was over at his place doing his taxes, and I mentioned your case to him. He took me out to his chicken coop and there they were, buried under a pile of straw in a corner. They're the bible on maritime law. You see these marks here?" he said, pointing to some white and gray smudges. "That's chickenshit."

"The whole thing's chickenshit," I said.

"There's some very interesting stuff in here," he said. "When you were first hired, did you sign shipping articles?"

"What are they?"

"All the rules and regulations you're subject to as a seaman. It's a contract between the ship's master and his crew. You should have signed them when you first went aboard, and again when you were transferred to the engineroom."

"I signed something, but it wasn't any set of rules and regulations."

"They were never read to you?"

"No."

"When you were fired, were you told why you were being discharged?" he asked.

"I wasn't told anything," I said. "Sparky had me sign two copies of my discharge papers, and then he told me to get off the ship. It was pretty obvious why."

"The captain wasn't present when you were discharged?"

"No. Where is this going?" I asked.

50

"The ship's master is required to have you sign the articles, and to permit you to read them or read them to you, before you ship out. If that isn't done, there may be no jurisdictional grounds to prosecute you. Moreover, if you commit an offense against the articles, the captain is required to make a complete entry in the ship's log, signed by the captain and at least one other crew member, the entry must be read to you by the captain, you have to be given a chance to respond, and your response must also be recorded in the log."

"That certainly wasn't done," I said.

"That might be grounds for dismissal," he said. "When the search party entered your room, did they ask permission?"

"Are you joking?"

"There you go again."

"No."

"Was the door closed?"

"Yes."

"Were you ever shown a search warrant?"

"No."

"We may also have grounds to argue an illegal search and seizure," he said. "I'm going to start by filing two motions, one for an outright dismissal and one for suppression of evidence. Maybe we won't have to go any further."

"Wouldn't that be nice?" I said.

"Wouldn't it?"

"Do you ever lose?" I asked.

"Oh, I lose cases all the time," he said. "But I win a lot more than I lose. What about your military service?" he asked.

"What about it?"

"You have an honorable discharge, don't you?"

"Yes."

"Anything else? Did you get any medals, commendations, things like that?"

"I've got three rows of battle ribbons. I made sergeant in twenty-one months. Purple Heart, meritorious mast, division commander's commendation, junk like that."

"Can you document it?"

"Why?"

"It might come in handy."

"I don't think so," I said.

"Why not?"

"Too weird."

"Care to explain?" said Richards.

"Look, we've got a government that's trying to burn me for less than half an ounce of pot, and I'm supposed to use a bunch of junk I got from that same government for committing murder and mayhem to get them to believe that I'm really a swell guy?"

"One uses whatever leverage one's got," he said.

"Not that. Not me."

"Do you want to win?"

"I've still got a passport, if it comes to that."

"Even if you're convicted, you might still keep your papers if your drug use is found to be experimental and the judge believes you won't do it again."

"'Youser, youser, I'm so sorry. I'll never smoke that terrible stuff again.' I'm sorry about a lot of things, Robert, but smoking marijuana isn't one of them. I'm not proud of what I did to get those decorations."

"You want to think it over?"

"Do I sound like I want to think it over?"

"Okay, suit yourself."

"I got arrested for armed robbery," I said. I told him what had happened in New York, including the fact that the liquor store owner had cleared us twenty minutes after we'd arrived at the police station, something Jim had found out subsequently. "They held us for another three and a half hours while they ran our names through every police computer in the world. Hell, if they picked us up, we must be guilty of something, right? We got copies of the 'Stop and Frisk' Reports they filed on us," I said, taking out my copy. "Listen to this. 'How long was person stopped? Forty minutes.' That's a lie. 'Was force used? No.' What do you call a cannon pointed straight between the eyes? 'Was person frisked? No.' That's a lie. 'Person was pointed out by witness as being involved in an armed robbery.' That's a lie. We never got within half a block of the store that got robbed, and the robbery was long over before we ever got to Jim's car. This is all lies. So I wrote to the police commissioner to complain, and this is what I get back."

I pulled out another sheet of paper, this one on New York City Police Department letterhead, and began to read: "'Records of this command indicate that on the evening of May 30th, 1974, you were accompanied to the Mid-Town Precinct North for the purpose of assisting the Anti-Crime Unit in a continuing investigation, which was concluded with negative results. The Commanding Officer of the precinct appreciates your cooperation and wishes to express his thanks for your actions. Sergeant Joseph Brunner, Administrative Officer.' Now isn't that interesting? Just a good citizen doing my civic duty."

"You don't like it?" said Richards. "Do something about it. Don't just sit around complaining about it."

"I spent four years trying to do something about it," I said. "I actually put on a coat and tie and went to places like the Swarthmore Rotary Club and the Nether Providence Chamber of Commerce. I actually thought they would listen to me. But the war's still going on. And nobody even cares anymore."

"Who's talking about the war?" Richards said. "I thought we were talking about you getting arrested for armed robbery."

"It's all connected," I said. "It's all the same system. But then, you've never been arrested for armed robbery, have you? You've never been indicted for conspiracy to blow up the Republican National Convention. And you make a pretty good living off the system, don't you, patching up the sorry bastards who get their arms and legs and noses caught in the gears."

"If you weren't always spoiling for a fight, you'd see that I see a lot more than you think I do."

"I wasn't always spoiling for a fight," I said. "I volunteered for the Marine Corps. I actually volunteered for Vietnam. Couldn't wait to do my civic duty."

"That's not spoiling for a fight?" he said.

"God damn it, Robert, you know what I mean."

"Why do you think I'm a defense attorney?" he said. "You think I wouldn't make a crackerjack prosecutor? You think I couldn't be a judge? Why do you think I took your case? Or George Martin's? I do make a pretty good living off the system, but every time I take a case to court and win, I change the system, too. This ought to be too obvious to need saying, but change doesn't happen overnight. You want to see another Bolshevik revolution? Another French revolution?"

"I want an American revolution," I said, "not some stupid merchant-class tax revolt."

"No, you don't," he said. "You know better than that."

"Do I?"

"Yes. Are the Russians better off for their revolution? What did the French get? Napoleon Bonaparte. At least we've got a system where change is possible. You make a commitment and you stick to it. You get beaten and you come back again. You get knocked down and you get up and keep going."

"You sound like my mother."

"Then she's a very wise woman," he said. "You ought to pay more attention to her. Sixty years ago, your mother couldn't vote—"

"She wasn't alive then."

"—Negroes couldn't vote. Lynchings were commonplace. There weren't any child labor laws, or fire codes. Twenty years ago, Negroes couldn't buy a cup of coffee at a lunchcounter."

"So now Frank Rizzo can stripsearch Black Panthers right on the street in front of the television cameras and get himself elected mayor of Philadelphia," I said.

"I'm not saying it's perfect," he said. "But it can be changed. It's changing right before your eyes."

"Smoke and mirrors, Robert. So a black man can get a cup of

coffee. Let him try to get a job. So women can vote, but watch any woman under fifty walk past a construction site on a summer day and listen to the reaction—"

"Hey, that's not the system," Richards said. "That's human nature. You think the same thing doesn't happen in the Soviet Union? And I wonder what would have happened to you and your friend if you'd been picked up for armed robbery in Minsk."

"The perfect comeback," I said. "Hey, it isn't perfect, but it's still the best system on earth, right?"

"But it's true," he said. "Show me a better one."

"It may be true," I said, "but that says more about the sorry state of humanity than it does about the virtues of America."

"What are you going to do with the rest of your life?" he said.

"I don't know," I said. "Why do you keep asking me that? Tell me something. Does this room make you dizzy?"

"What?"

"Everything's crooked," I said. "The floor tilts. The ceiling tilts. The windows are cockeyed. It makes me dizzy."

"Makes me feel like Thomas Jefferson," he said. "Monticello's just like this. Well, almost. It was built the same year as this house. Jefferson wrote the Declaration of Independence."

"I know that," I said.

"Remarkable document."

"If you're a white man."

"You manage to find it everywhere, don't you?" he said.

"What's there is there."

"You think you're the only one who sees it?" he said.

"I don't see you losing any sleep over it."

"Lord, grant me the strength to change what I can, the patience to accept what I can't—"

"—and the wisdom to know the difference. My mother used to have that taped to our refrigerator."

"Didn't seem to make much of an impression, did it?" he said.

"Whatever," I said, shrugging.

"Why don't you go to law school?" said Richards.

"What?"

"Why don't you go to law school? You'd make a good lawyer. You like to argue."

"No thanks."

"Are you going to be a forklift driver for the rest of your life?"

"Why not?" I said.

*   *   *

The warehouse where I worked was attached to a do-it-yourself home remodeling store called Panel Emporium. Daniel Kaufman was the store manager, which is how I got the job. He'd started as a manager-trainee two years earlier and rapidly worked his way up. Our store was one of eleven Panel Emporiums scattered throughout Philadelphia and the Delaware Valley that sold every kind of paneling known to the civilized world, along with floor and ceiling tile, toilets, kitchen counters, paint, molding, screws and bolts, roller brushes with handles thirteen feet long, bathtubs, cabinets, sinks, gadgets, light switches, and microwave ovens—this was back in the days when it was commonly believed that if you used one, you would turn into green slime and begin to glow while you waited for your coffee to get hot, but people bought them anyway.

Customers would pick out what they wanted from the showroom, pay for it, then drive around back and pick up the big stuff from the warehouse. Sometimes it would be a nice-looking woman in her thirties who would flirt with me while I loaded her car. Sometimes she'd tip me. Most of the customers were Handy-Andy middle-aged men with baggy pants and belts with special loops for tape measures, or pale housewives with too many children. My favorites were the ones who bought flakeboard panels from Taiwan. These were on permanent special at $2.99 a four-by-eight-foot sheet. The people who bought them were always stupid, cheap, or both. They'd come into the warehouse asking for twenty or thirty sheets at a time. I always kept a sheet ready as a demonstrator.

"Are you sure this is what you want?" I'd ask, snapping off a corner with my thumb and forefinger to show them how brittle and weak it was.

"This is the stuff that's on special, right?"

"You get what you pay for," I'd say.

"Yeh, that's what I want."

One day, a man with balding red hair and a potbelly told me to tie twenty sheets of flakeboard to the roof of his car, a Plymouth sedan.

"You can't carry that much on your roof," I told him. "The stuff's too brittle. It'll break apart if you hit a bump."

"Just get it up there," he said. "I'm in a hurry."

"Really, you can't carry that much. There's no way I can tie it so it won't break."

"You just get it up there. I'll tie it myself."

"Okay," I said, and I did, and he did, and then he drove away. fifteen minutes later, he was back. There was nothing on the roof of his car but some loose loops of rope. He was livid. He wanted more panels.

"You gotta pay for 'em first," I said.

"Goddamn shit. What kind of cheap shit are you selling? You owe me twenty goddamned panels."

I called Daniel on the intercom. "You'd better get back here," I said.

Daniel enjoyed working in sales because he enjoyed people. Especially idiots. The man began to give Daniel an animated version of what had happened.

"Please don't swear in my store," Daniel said. "You're behaving very badly."

"Who the hell do you think you are?" the man roared at Daniel.

"I'm the store manager," Daniel said. "I have a personal relationship with the Havertown police chief. Now why do you think we owe you twenty panels?"

"Because this—this guy here refused to tie them down for me and I lost the whole load."

"And why did my warehouseman refuse to tie the panels on for you?" Daniel asked. The man didn't say anything. "Because he told you that you couldn't carry that many, didn't he? He showed you how brittle flakeboard is, and then he told you that if you tried to carry that many on the roof of your car, you'd lose the whole load, didn't he? And you lost the whole load. That's not my fault, and it's not his fault. It's your fault. If you want more, come around front and pay for them. If you don't want to pay for them, go away."

The man turned redder than the few strands of hair left on his head, then he jumped into his car and drove away, squealing his tires.

Most people paid more attention to me. I got very good at loading paneling onto cars and trucks and vans and stationwagons and tying it down securely, knowing what was safe to carry on which kinds of vehicles and what was not. I learned to whip my forklift around the crowded warehouse like Parnelli Jones at the Brickyard. The forklift had rear wheel steering, which meant it could turn on a dime and give you nine cents change. I could zoom down the aisles with a load of twenty Hawaiian Luau panels—top of the line, $18.99 a sheet—turn ninety degrees at the end of an aisle without slowing down, and make for the garage area at full speed where the customer would be waiting. Then I'd watch the customer's eyes get round and white as I bore down on the family stationwagon with $379.80 worth of paneling and four tons of forklift.

I was sitting on top of a stack of ceiling tile one afternoon, dirty and tired, having just unloaded and stacked an entire semi-trailer full of tile that had come in that day, when Damn Meddlesome swaggered into the warehouse acting important. That wasn't his real name, but it was close enough. He was one of the company's vice presidents.

The president of Panel Emporium, Incorporated, Gary Edelman, was a young man in his late thirties who had parlayed a neighborhood garage sale into a multi-million dollar empire in only ten years on nothing but innate business acumen. His one flaw was the people he kept around him. They were all relatives and boyhood friends. His two younger brothers were vice presidents. Damn Meddlesome had given Edelman his very own Boy Scout knife when they were both ten. Or his favorite frog. Something like that. Edelman was too nice a guy to realize that he had gotten where he was not because of the guys who had been there from the beginning, but in spite of them.

Damn Meddlesome strutted up and down for awhile, flapping his arms while Daniel followed him with a bemused look on his face, as if he were watching a stand-up comic and had not yet decided if what he was hearing was funny enough to laugh at. Then Damn Meddlesome stalked over to a small pile of debris I had been sweeping up when the tile had arrived and, pointing at me, said to Daniel, "Have that boy clean this up."

That night I wrote a letter to Gary Edelman. I explained the circumstances by which I had come to be sitting on a stack of Armstrong tile while that pile of trash lay on the floor. I pointed out to him that I was an honorably discharged Marine sergeant and held a Bachelor of Arts degree.

"I am not a boy," I said. "If Panel Emporium values intelligent, capable employees, you might do well to instruct your representatives to remove their heads from their bottoms."

Three days later, Edelman offered to promote me to manager-trainee. He called me on the telephone at work. I told him I didn't want to be a manager. I liked driving a forklift. What I wanted was fulltime hours and a pay raise. "Consider it done," he said. Finally I could buy another car.

*   *   *

I'd sold the only car I'd ever owned to Daniel more than a year earlier for the cost of a one-way ticket on the San Francisco Zephyr and a small stake to live on while I looked for a ship. Once I got a ship, I figured, I'd never need a car again. Now I found myself stranded on the beach. Being without a car was a kind of purgatory. One's soul was encumbered with leg irons. And as added punishment, because Daniel was my friend and boss and I saw him often, I was made to ride in the very car that had once been my ticket to freedom. I had loved that car.

It was a red Volkswagen bug. I'd bought it the day after I got home from Vietnam. When I first went to Vietnam, I'd been saving my money for a shared life with Jenny, the girl from the neighboring town I'd met three months before joining the Marines. Hormones raging, we had necked and dry-humped our way through the last three months of my senior year in high school, knowing I would be leaving for boot camp and Vietnam right after graduation. We would often keep at it until the windows of my mother's Studebaker Lark were so steamed you couldn't see out of them and I had come in my pants and we were both drenched with sweat. But I had never so much as unhooked her bra or palmed her sweet mound. She was a good Catholic girl who went to confession every week, and she couldn't do it, or anything like it, until she was married. By the time I'd left for boot camp, we were sure we'd be married when I came home from Vietnam.

We'd kept it up for more than a year. Through boot camp and advanced infantry training. Through a quick succession of training assignments and then staging. Through the first seven months of Vietnam, where I burned down houses and shot people and began to understand dimly that I'd made a bad mistake and might die for it. She wrote every day. Her letters were perfumed. They were gay and full of longing. My world was coming apart, and she was the only stable thing left in it. But I was far away, and we were very young. One day her letters stopped coming. One final letter arrived six weeks later. After that, I was saving for a car.

It had cost me $2,021: tax, tags, and drive it off the showroom floor. Every penny I'd saved in 395 days of war. When people asked me why I'd bought a red one, I would always tell them, "because I bought it with blood money," and no one understood that I did not mean it as a joke. I put 18,000 miles on it in the first ten weeks.

Before I sold it five years later, I'd driven to California twice, to Florida three times, to Colorado and Canada, Chillicothe, Chattanooga, and Charleston. I toured America by interstate highway.

There were demonstrations in every city. There were American flags flying proudly in the windows of gas stations from Providence to Pocatello. Bumper stickers threatened, "America: Love it or leave it," and bell-bottomed couples high on LSD stood beside the road with their thumbs out. Walter Cronkite talked to every television set west of Newfoundland and east of Anchorage, and the headlines were the same in the St. Louis *Post-Dispatch* as they were in the Atlanta *Constitution*. I don't know why, but I kept thinking I could outrun America. As long as I had gas in the tank. As long as I had asphalt in front of me. I drove relentlessly.

But I couldn't outrun it. In 1968, the Reverend Doctor Martin Luther King, Junior, was shot dead and America's cities, already tinderboxes of Black frustration, caught fire and burned. Robert Kennedy ruthlessly stole Eugene McCarthy's thunder, only to be ruthlessly murdered for his trouble, plunging the Democratic party into the hands of Lyndon Johnson's lapdog and the country's yearning for peace into the hands of Richard Nixon. In 1971, broken-hearted veterans hurled their medals back at the Congress in whose name they had been given while Congress cowered behind a cyclone fence it had erected to keep its members safe from the unclean rabble that had done its bidding. The *Pentagon Papers*, commissioned by McNamara himself though never intended for public consumption, finally revealed what any dumb grunt could have told you after ninety days in Vietnam, that the war was a madness. And none of it had mattered. The war went on like a ballpeen hammer in the hands of a steady workman. Henry Kissinger announced that peace was at hand, King Richard the Milhous was re-elected, the Christmas bombs fell on Hanoi's Bach Mai Hospital, and no matter how far or how fast I drove, I couldn't get far enough away.

I didn't speak any language but English, which eliminated most of the world. I had no skill with which to support myself in Canada

61

or Australia or New Zealand. But there was still another option short of the one Max Harris had chosen.

In the summer of 1969, between the Marine Corps and college, I had spent some time as a deckhand aboard a small Irish coastal freighter. I'd gone to England intending to hitchhike around Europe for the summer before college started, but I hadn't been there two weeks when I'd met four young seamen one night in a bar in Liverpool. They were the deck crew of the M/V *Marizell*. After a few beers and a few games of darts, we'd all concluded that I ought to go sailing. The captain, who'd been sailing so long his first ship had been a windjammer, was less enthusiastic, but after much cajoling and pleading from his youthful crew, he'd finally agreed.

For six weeks, we'd crisscrossed the Irish Sea between Dublin and Liverpool, hauling cotton bales and chicken feed, steel girders and tractors. General cargo. That summer Neil Armstrong walked on the moon, taking one small step for man, one giant step for mankind. My shipmates thought it a wondrous thing. I thought it a wondrous thing that a C-47 gunship could fire 18,000 bullets a minute, making human bodies instantly unrecognizable, but I hadn't told them that. Their attention was all on Northern Ireland, where fifty years of Irish anger had exploded in blood that summer. The Yanks' war in Vietnam was no concern of theirs, which was fine with me. On a ship far from America and its filthy war in Vietnam, I was in paradise.

So when I'd run out of places to drive, I had sold the little red VW to Daniel and set out on a different highway. There I'd met the righteous Henry Kyle and his humorless minions.

But with longer hours and better pay at Panel Emporium, I could buy another car. I could feel the first downy feathers of flight tickling the back of my neck. At least I would have mobility back. I bought a used 1972 MG Midget, yellow with black convertible top and black leather interior. It was a tiny machine, just two seats and an engine. It looked faster than it drove on the flat, but it maneuvered like a bat and you sat so low to the road, it felt like you were blasting along on rails. It had a tachometer. As light as a bird, it swooped and soared and floated on the wind. I loved it.

A few days after I got it, a heavy rain washed the cardboard temporary tag off. Either that or someone tore it off that night. I didn't think much about it. I went to a justice of the peace and got an affidavit attesting that the car was legally registered and awaiting permanent license plates. I got stopped several times, but each time I produced my affidavit and that had satisfied the cops. Then one evening after work, I drove over to visit a friend in Maple Shade, New Jersey.

*   *   *

About a mile from Kathy's place, I stopped for gas. A Maple Shade cop was parked at the gas station, and I expected him to come over and ask about my missing license plate, but he didn't. I pulled out and turned the corner. I could see Kathy's apartment building. Just then two cop cars came barreling around the corner in front of me and, driving abreast, headed straight for me. In the rearview mirror, I could see two more cars approaching from behind. I stopped right where I was.

Small town cops are a terrifying phenomenon. They're the guys who couldn't meet the minimum mental, physical, or psychological standards for the state police academies, the guys who were army supply clerks during the Korean War, the G-Man Wannabees and Lee Marvin Fan Club members, gunslingers and survivalists and torturers of small furry animals. They imagine their snug little communities besieged by wild Indians and Eastern European anarchists, and they imagine themselves as defenders of the True Cross. They are armed and dangerous. Six cops flew out of their cars and came at me from all directions, guns drawn and pointed at my head.

"Out of the car. Easy!" one of them shouted. He had sergeant's stripes on his sleeves. "Keep your hands where I can see 'em!"

I opened the door very slowly and eased out of the car as gently as I could manage, which is no mean trick when your rear end is only six inches off the road and your feet are thrust straight out in front of you, which is how you are seated when you drive an MG Midget. He immediately spun me around and pushed me down on the engine cover, so that I had no choice but to put my hands out to break my fall, causing me to "assume the position" automatically. The cop kicked my feet even farther apart, until I was stretched nearly horizontal. Then he patted me down.

"I can explain the license plate," I said.

"Shut up!" barked Sergeant Bilko. Then the questions: who was I, where did I live, where was I going? "Stand up slowly and take your wallet out," he said. "Driver's license. Registration." I handed him both, along with the affidavit. "It's illegal to drive a car without plates," he said.

"That's a sworn affidavit from a district judge," I said.

"This is from Pennsylvania," Sergeant Bilko sneered. "It doesn't mean a thing in New Jersey." The other cops had holstered their pistols, but kept their hands on the stocks and didn't move.

"I was just stopped Saturday night on I-295 by a New Jersey state trooper," I said, "He seemed to think it was okay."

"Oh, a smart ass," he said. "We got a smart ass here."

"You wanna search the car? You want me to open the trunk for you?"

"You look scruffy," said Sergeant Bilko.

"You see these scars?" I said, pointing to my neck and chin. "Marine Corps. Vietnam." Actually, I'd gotten those particular scars in a car accident when I was fifteen, but I wasn't about to pull my pants down in the middle of the street and show him the ones I was really talking about. "I've got a right to look any way I please. I earned it."

"You're a disgrace to the uniform you wore," he said, as if he were biting on something unpleasant. I wanted to tell him that if he thought I was a disgrace, then I must be doing something right. But he had a gun. And a badge. So did his pals. Shot while resisting arrest. I kept my mouth shut. "Get out of here," said Sergeant

64

Bilko, stiffening his jaw and giving me his best imitation of Marshal Dillon. "Keep going till you're out of New Jersey. And don't come back."

No doubt he suspected I was a member of the Symbionese Liberation Army. That February, 1974, they'd kidnapped nineteen-year-old Patricia Hearst, daughter and heiress of William Randolph Hearst with a Roman numeral after his name, who owned a publishing empire and whose grandfather had invented yellow journalism and Teddy Roosevelt and started the Spanish-American War. The SLA felt Hearst the father didn't deserve to be so rich, which was probably true because most rich people get that way mostly by taking other people's money, so they'd kidnapped Hearst the daughter.

The SLA ordered Hearst the father to feed all the poor people in Berkeley, Caifornia, if he ever wanted to see Hearst the daughter alive again. He did that, but then Hearst the daughter said she was embarrassed to be so rich and decided to enlist in the SLA. She changed her name to Tania, not coincidentally the name of the late Che Guevara's mistress, and started robbing banks. With Tania's conversion to The Cause, the ranks of the SLA swelled to six or seven members, whom the media and law enforcement officials insisted on calling "troopers."

Kidnapping is a particularly cruel crime, and it must have been no fun for Mr. and Mrs. Hearst, no matter how rich they were or how they had gotten their money. Still, one had to admire the SLA's spunk. Much of what they said about the system was true, and they weren't just sitting around complaining about it. They were, like small-town cops, armed and dangerous. But a half-dozen college drop-outs and petty hoods with delusions of grandeur represented no more of a threat to the good people of Maple Shade, New Jersey, than any street gang in nearby Camden—except that this particular gang had reached right into the sanctity of the American home and plucked out a white girl. Sergeant Bilko was not going to fail his community. I had to go, even if there was no law under the sun that required me to do so.

*   *   *

I had the next day off and so did Daniel. Sarah was going with a girlfriend to look at dead cows and other animals fashioned into footwear, so Daniel and I decided to drive the MG over to New Jersey to explore the Pine Barrens. Stretching from Browns Mills south to Hammonton, the Pine Barrens were an incongruously pristine wilderness smack in the middle of the Northeast industrial corridor, almost unchanged since the earliest arrival of the Europeans: Swedes, later Dutch.

Blackbeard the Pirate had used the narrow rivers meandering through the Pine Barrens as hideouts from the British navy and hiding places for booty, so the local legends went. An ironworks at Batsto had forged local low-grade ore into cannonballs for George Washington's Continental Army. The locals themselves were sparsely scattered through the trackless stands of scrub cedar that turned twisting streams a deep red. There were towns like Jenkins and Sweetwater on the map, and they were eerier than ghost towns because people still lived in them, many eking out a kind of hunter-gatherer existence much like that of Appalachian hillbillies, though there were no hills to speak of between Mount Holly, northeast of Camden, and Cape May at the eastern tip of the Delaware Estuary, where South Jersey finally slides off the continent into the Atlantic Ocean.

Upscale retirement communities and shopping malls were inexorably eroding the edges of the Pine Barrens, but the heart of the place was still protected as a state forest. Daniel and I followed a series of ever smaller roads that took us deep into the barrens until we were swooshing along on a narrow sand track barely wide enough even for the Midget. The rear end swayed gently as the tires scrambled for purchase in the loose sand, giving the car and us a feeling of floating, and at times the wheel ruts became so deep that we'd bottom out and I'd have to steer to one side or the other, riding the hump in the center of the road and one edge of the forest, dodging branches and tree trunks.

66

It was a hot, clear day and we had the top down. Cedar fronds slapped at the windscreen, and now and then a bird would rise up indignantly and dart deeper into the trees. We didn't really get lost because none of these sand tracks was on the map anyway and we had nowhere in particular to go. Once we stopped at a bridge over a deep stream and took off our clothes and went swimming. The red water was sweet and clean. Nowhere else between Boston and Richmond was there water like this. One could almost imagine a time when the whole of North America smelled and tasted like this. It made the heart ache.

We drove for hours, saying little. Mostly Daniel made stupid remarks and offhand generalizations about the human condition that were usually correct.

"Presidents are always assholes," he said. "If they weren't, they wouldn't be presidents. Nothing special about this one."

This was in response to my complaint that New Jersey Representative Peter Rodino's House Judiciary Committee was taking its sweet time getting around to the obvious. As the evidence mounted against Nixon through the spring of 1974, a palpable tension had fallen over the whole of the nation, with the exception of Daniel. Even the true believers, who had come to understand that Nixon was not, after all, the Messiah, sank into a kind of terror when at last confronted with the reality that he was finished. It was much like a death watch. People wanted the end to come because the drawn-out vigil forced them to reflect upon their own mortality, yet they feared the fall of the president of the United States of America would bring with it the collapse of civilization as we know it.

Though Saigon had not yet fallen, anyone with anything between the ears more sophisticated than a pinball machine understood that we had been sent packing by a ragtag band of fishsucking farmers, most of them under five and a half feet tall and light enough to throw out with the garbage. All our glorious technology and spitshine get-go had been powerless to stop them. Few Americans considered the meaning of the British capture and destruction of Washington, D.C., not having been alive during the War of 1812, and thus they believed that nothing like our national humiliation in Indochina had ever happened before.

And now, even before the Red Hordes had gobbled up the Pearl of the Orient and sent the American ambassador scurrying to the rooftop to catch the last helicopter home like some middle-class commuter chasing a train, the president himself, the head of state, the very embodiment of the people, was about to be brought down. No American president had been impeached since Andrew Johnson, and no one remembered that, not having been alive in 1868. It was too much to bear. Anarchy would be loosed upon the land. The bra-burning feminists and mad dogs of hedonism would run wild in the streets. Women and children into the lifeboats. Every man for himself.

The Rodino Committee, caught between the palpable fear of their constituents and their own desperate fear that Nixon's indiscretions would eventually lead to the general realization that there was nothing so unusual about Nixon after all, moved ahead with glacial haste, wringing their hands and making soft bleating noises.

I wanted to see the buttons cut from Nixon's uniform and the epaulets torn from his shoulders. It was payback time, and he was as deserving a candidate as ever there was. No more Checkers speeches. No more honest Republican broadcloth coats. Just this once, let some sonofabitch who's held all the aces feel what it's like to hold nothing.

At every fork in the sandy track, we turned left, working our way slowly north and east. Then without warning, we came upon an astonishing sight. The road suddenly straightened and widened and passed by a neat parking area big enough for several dozen cars, like a small unpaved paradeground. In the center of it stood a stone obelisk, like a monument in a town square or a city park except that this was miles from anywhere. Several bouquets of fresh flowers had recently been left at the monument's base. They were not yet wilted. We stopped the car and got out.

The monument had been erected in memory of Emilio Carranza by the Mexican-American Friendship Association. Carranza, a Mexican pilot, had crashed on this spot in 1928 while attempting to fly non-stop from New York City to Mexico City as a gesture of Mexican-American friendship. Found dead in the wreckage of his airplane, he had flown less than seventy miles.

"He should have known better," I said. First the Texans decided they liked Americans better than Mexicans and took Texas from Mexico. Then James Polk decided he liked Americans better than Mexicans and took the rest of the Southwest from Mexico. Then Woodrow Wilson decided he didn't like Pancho Villa, and took Vera Cruz and burned it. Even a cursory study of history suggested that there never had been such a thing as Mexican-American friendship. "He never had a chance," I said.

*   *   *

There were no tabernacles in Tabernacle, New Jersey, not that we could see, but there was a gas station. "If Senor Carranza had been driving instead of flying," Daniel said when we stopped to fill up the car, "he could have stopped here for repairs and saved himself a lot of trouble."

"Gimme five dollars," I said.

"Goddamned Arabs," said Daniel.

In the wake of the Yom Kippur War, Arab suppliers of crude oil had called an embargo in protest of U.S. support of Israel, causing gasoline shortages for the first time since the Second World War, which resulted in long lines at closed pumps and people getting into fistfights and sometimes shooting each other over a gallon of gasoline, which is perhaps better than shooting somebody for his sneakers, but not by much. The Arabs finally reopened the tap and gas lines had gradually disappeared, but by then the price of gasoline had risen to two and a half times its pre-embargo price. In the months that followed, it had become clear that it would not be coming down.

69

"There was no shortage," I told Daniel. "While people were killing each other in gas lines, tankers were riding anchors all over Long Beach harbor. They were low in the water, waiting to be unloaded. Nobody seemed in a big hurry. The oil companies faked the whole thing so they could jack up the price."

"The Arabs raised the price," said Daniel.

"Not as much as the oil companies did. Besides, we've been stealing them blind for forty years. It's about time we paid up."

"They wouldn't have any oil if it weren't for us," Daniel said. "They've been riding around on camels for forty generations and didn't even know the stuff was there."

He had been in Israel during the Six Day War in June 1967, a war its name accurately described and in which the Israeli Defense Forces had stomped the daylights out of the Egyptian, Syrian, and Jordanian armies and taken the Sinai Peninsula, the Golan Heights, Gaza and the Strip, the West Bank, and that most holy of cities, Jerusalem. I'd been an eighteen-year-old lance corporal, fading slowly in the red dust of Vietnam, it being the dry season then, and we'd read the news in *Stars and Stripes* and envied the Israelis their swiftness and their victory, shaking our heads and looking out over the berm across the empty paddyfields stretching to the Annamese Cordillero. Daniel had been living in Israel with his family, his father, a chemical engineer, having taken a job there when Daniel was eleven.

A high school boy too young to fight, he had taken delight in the swagger and startling might of the Israelis. Later he had found an Egyptian helmet abandoned in the desert, and seen the blackened hulls of Egyptian tanks, and he too had been envious. Back in the United States for college, he had enrolled in the Marine Corps Platoon Leaders Class, a two-summer program that would give him a commission as a second lieutenant on graduation from college.

But by then it was 1969. The Tet Offensive a year earlier had put the lie to General William Westmoreland's light at the end of the tunnel, and it was apparent that the American war in Vietnam

70

would be concluded neither swiftly nor victoriously. It was the summer 400,000 kids had come together at Woodstock, New York, to celebrate rock-and-roll in the Age of Aquarius, an age that was already dying, though they had not known it at the time. The first six-week session at Quantico, Virginia, had been enough to convince Daniel that the Marines were not the Israeli Defense Forces and the Vietnamese were not the Arabs, and he had not returned the following summer for the final installment.

"The money," I said. "Give it to me."

"Goddamned Arabs," said Daniel, handing over a $5 bill.

On the way home, we drove well out of our way to see if the old coot up on Route 206 was still there. I'd been driving to the beach one day in the summer of 1969 when a roadside junkyard quite out of the ordinary caught my attention. A chain-link fence surrounded the yard, which was all grass like a lawn, and lined up in neat rows were plows and harrows, old tractors, truck rims, buses, engine blocks, pumps and generators of all sizes, hubcaps, the grass neatly mown around each item, the only uncut grass growing up through the machinery. A small shanty built against a mobile home stood near an open gate in the fence.

What stopped me, though, was the signs. The place looked like a Burma Shave advertisement that had overdosed on Miracle-Gro. All along the fence facing the highway stood painted white signs with black block-printed lettering. Some of them had large lettering with only a few words: "Stop Nixon's Immoral War In Vietnam" and "No More Taxes For War." Some had small lettering with lots of words: "It is the people's right to refuse to give our children's lives in a criminal war. By no international treaty or provision of the constitution do we have the right to invade another country and dictate what its government shall be. Our government is in violation of its own Nuremberg Principles. Our national leaders are criminals."

Five or six other cars were parked on the shoulder, their occupants slowly walking the length of the fence, reading signs. A bearded old man looking like Gabby Hayes stood in front of the shanty. "They're trying to run me out," he said to no one in particular. "Come sign my petition." He had told me that he'd owned his junkyard—used parts business, he'd called it—for twenty-three years without one complaint. But when he'd put up the signs, the township had suddenly found his establishment in violation of fifteen zoning and safety ordinances. They were trying to close him down.

"Man's got a right to his opinion," he had said, pushing the petition at me. "It's in the Bill of Rights. The First Amendment. I can read."

I had signed his petition. Several more times in the next couple of years, I had driven by. Each time he'd been there, signs and all. But that had been three or four years ago. Daniel and I went to see if he was still there, but he wasn't. There was only a field of tall grass. No doubt, it had all been perfectly legal.

"When the president does it, that means it's not illegal," Nixon had said. He had wanted to enlist the Teamsters Union to deal with the antiwar demonstrators. "They, they've got guys who'll go in and knock their heads off," he had said. "Murderers. They're gonna beat the shit out of those people." Had he reached into New Jersey and plucked Gabby Hayes from the side of the road?

But there were little Nixons all over America. Little Nixons and little Joe McCarthys and little Attila the Huns. More of them than anyone wanted except them. The township fathers would have needed no help from the Big Dick.

"First we shoot the lawyers," I said as we turned around and headed back down the road.

"The lawyers are all in Congress," said Daniel. "Zoning and safety are regulated by the states. State legislatures are packed with insurance agents."

"We shoot the insurance agents right after we shoot the lawyers."

"Better not shoot your lawyer," said Daniel.

"If we'd shot the lawyers in the first place, I wouldn't need one."

"Then who'd protect you from the righteous Henry Kyle and

his humorless minions?" said Daniel. I looked over at him. "I've heard you say it often enough."

"We shoot them, too," I said.

"That's just how they feel about you."

"I know."

*   *   *

That night, Sarah, Daniel, and I had dinner with Daniel's brother Sam and his wife, Jan. Daniel and Sam were twins, though they did not look at all alike. Each was a big man, but Daniel had coarse dark hair all over his body. He had to shave all the way down to his collar. He looked like a caveman with clothes. Sam was a big blond teddy bear. He and Jan had met at a dude ranch in Montana where they'd both worked one summer, and they had married as soon as they'd graduated from college.

The wedding had been at Jan's parents' house in Coral Gables, Florida, a waterfront place with a sailboat tied up at the slip and a swimming pool in the backyard. Jan's father was a retired air force pilot. He made the mistake of saying he thought the protesters at Kent State had gotten exactly what they'd been looking for, and I made the mistake of saying I thought the president of the United States, the governor of Ohio, the commanding general of the Ohio National Guard, the commander of the detachment dispatched to Kent State, and the company commander of the men who had fired the bullets ought to be hung by the neck for murder. Then we'd all ended up in the swimming pool, the groom and the father of the bride still in their tuxedoes, the bride in her wedding gown. "Great wedding!" Daniel had said, up to his waist in water, a glass of champagne in one hand.

Sam worked for the Pennsylvania Crime Commission investigating allegations of widespread graft and corruption in the Philadelphia Police Department. Cops breaking into warehouses and stealing the goods they were supposed to be protecting. Cops making drug busts, then selling or keeping part of the evidence.

Cops taking cash payments instead of issuing traffic tickets. Cops taking payoffs from bar owners to overlook violations of state liquor control board regulations.

This last was a good scam. LCB regulations were so complicated that it was impossible to run an establishment serving or selling liquor without being in violation of one statute or another, no matter how conscientious one was. If you didn't pay, you lost your liquor license. And everybody got a piece of the payoff. The bagman got some. His partner got some. The other members of his squad got some. His sergeant got some. In some cases, lieutenants and even captains got some. And some of them were really getting some. Some of the seedier bar owners provided women as well as money.

The investigation had recently picked up steam when undercover state troopers turned one young cop. They had caught him and his partner on film. They had shown him the film. He hadn't taken any money himself, he'd explained. He had only been on the force ten months. He had been told by his partner, a veteran of nineteen years, that this was the way it was. Go along to get along. If he didn't want the money, that was his business, but don't rock the boat because you've got a long voyage ahead of you.

Knowledge of the act makes you as guilty as if you had taken the money yourself, they had told him. They had offered him a choice. Stay on the beat, carry a wire, turn state's evidence, and we'll give you immunity and a new identity under the witness protection program. Refuse and be prosecuted. Now he had a new name and lived in a different state and would spend the rest of his life in fear of his former fellow officers. Whenever he came to Philadelphia to testify, he was never without two armed state justice department special agents. Not even in his hotel bathroom.

Confronted with the crime commission's findings, the district attorney had declined to act, arguing that an investigation of the police would jeopardize his working relationship with the very people he depended upon for all his other criminal prosecutions, though there were those who believed that the real reason the district attorney refused to act was because he was in the mayor's pocket. A state judge had therefore empaneled a special investigating grand jury and the state justice department had authorized a special prosecutor to pursue the investigation. Shortly thereafter, the judge had added an investigation of political corruption in Philadelphia to the grand jury's charge. Sam was in the process of transferring from the crime commission's staff to the special prosecutor's office.

Neither agency was authorized to investigate charges of police brutality, but people came to them anyway because they had nowhere else to go. Sam was full of stories. Motorists beaten senseless for running a red light. Teenagers beaten while walking home from a high school orchestra concert. Husbands beaten and arrested for defending their wives from verbal assault of the grossest sexual bluntness. Heroin addicts beaten to death. The white folks were always the most amazed. They never expected it. When Sam told them he couldn't help, they would carry on about their right to petition the government for redress of grievances and various other curiosities found in high school civics books.

Daniel roared at each story. "Pound sand!" he'd say. "Pass the peas."

"Wait till it happens to you," I said.

"Not me," Daniel said.

Sam and I looked at each other. Sam and Daniel's father, a World War Two navy veteran who had made a prosperous life for himself and his family by hard work and brilliance, had had an experience three years earlier that had changed his way of seeing. Curious to know why his sons' friends were all so angry at the country that had given him such opportunity, he had ventured to Washington to observe one of the big antiwar demonstrations. There he had been caught in the midst of a police riot. "Those kids weren't doing anything wrong," he had said, coming home with twelve stitches in his head, courtesy of a police baton. Sam had subsequently gone to work for the Pennsylvania Crime Commission. Daniel sold Hawaiian Luau and flakeboard from Taiwan.

"Not you?" said Sam.

"You're wasting your time, Sam," said Daniel. "You're spending the taxpayers' money, and you won't get one significant conviction. It'll all blow over in a year or two."

*   *   *

On the day of my hearing, Richards met me at the train station and we took the train into Philadelphia. I was wearing a sport coat and tie.

"What's that?" Richards asked, pointing to the pin on my lapel.

"The Purple Heart," I said.

"I thought that was too weird."

"I'm not throwing myself on the mercy of the court," I said. "It doesn't hurt to wear it."

"I see you got a haircut, too."

"I figured that wouldn't hurt, either," I said. "My mother did it."

"If you were getting one cut, why didn't you cut the rest of them?"

"Ha, ha," I said. "I got thrown out of New Jersey last week."

"New Jersey?"

"Yes."

"The whole state?"

"Apparently," I said. "Wyatt Earp said I looked scruffy. Told me to get out of Dodge." I told Richards what had happened.

"Well, why do you go around dressed for trouble?"

"Blue jeans and a denim jacket is dressed for trouble?"

"Apparently."

"This is America, isn't it? I need to ask the Maple Shade Police Department what their dress code is?"

"I'm just being realistic," said Richards. "Who are you hurting by running your head against a wall?"

"For chrissake, Robert, we're talking about blue jeans here. Levi Strauss. The California Gold Rush. How American can you

76

get? I can't wear blue jeans?"

"You're oversimplifying," he said. "And you know it."

"'Live Free Or Die.' That's what it says on New Hampshire license plates. Did you know that?"

"Sometimes I think you want to make your life as hard as you can," he said. "If you can't find something to be angry about, you just keep pushing until you do."

"I don't have to push very hard. Did you see what Kliendeinst got? Thirty days and a hundred dollar fine—suspended. Magruder gets ten months in Allenwood. They've got tennis courts at Allenwood. And conjugal suites. Kalmbach gets six to eighteen months at Lompoc. They've got a driving range and nine-hole golf course at Lompoc. And nude sunbathing. Meanwhile, some kid in Texas gets ten years' hard time for possession of two joints."

"Nixon won't last much longer," he said. "That ought to cheer you up."

"And then we'll get Gerald R. Ford. Who elected him?"

"Show me another country in the world where a sitting head of state can be removed from office without a civil war or a revolution."

"He's not gone yet," I said. "Besides, more than one British prime minister has been thrown out of office for a whole lot less than Nixon's pulled. And what about Portugal? They just got rid of a fifty-year dictatorship and didn't shed a drop of blood doing it. We're not so damned special, Robert. Better than some, worse than others."

"That's the biggest concession I've ever heard you make," he said.

"And what about you? You challenged me to show you another country where a sitting head of state can be removed without bloodshed, and I've just named two."

"Actually, the queen is the head of state in Britain."

"Jesus."

"But your point is well taken. We do have a habit of inflating our place in the cosmos."

"You've noticed."

"I told you, I notice more than you think I do. Still, two countries."

"Are you keeping score? I'm not responsible for what happens in Rhodesia. I don't pay taxes in Luxembourg. When the president of the United States calls the dictator of Nicaragua a great friend of democracy, he's doing it in my name. And then they eat a state dinner that I paid for. Then there's a couple of million dead Indochinese."

"It always comes back to that, doesn't it?" he said.

"That's only where it started. You think I'm just a casualty of war?"

"No, but I do think you need to figure out what you're going to do with the rest of your life."

"I'm already doing it," I said. I reached into the folder I was carrying and pulled out a copy of the book Jim Best had edited. "There's some poems of mine in here. I was going to give it to you on the way home."

He took the book and leafed through it, stopping to read a few times. "You want to be a poet," he said.

"I am a poet."

"How many people read poetry?"

"Not many," I said.

"You think you're going to change anything writing poetry? Do you want to have influence? Do you want to change things?"

"Maybe I don't think things can be changed."

"Go to law school," he said. "What I do changes things. We're a nation of laws and lawyers. That's reality. And it's not such a bad thing. Wallace Stevens was a lawyer."

"We're here," I said. We got off the train, took the Market Street subway to Second Street, then walked the two blocks over to the customs building and went up to the courtroom. There were four tables like you'd find in a high school biology class, arranged in a square. Jeffries showed us to our table. A Coast Guard enlisted man sat to our right with a dictaphone. To our left sat a young Coast Guard officer. "This is Lieutenant John Blavitt," said Jeffries, "He'll be handling the case for the government."

"Lieutenant junior grade," I said.

Blavitt stood up and shook hands with Richards. He had a baby face, and couldn't have been much older than me.

"Good luck to you," Blavitt said, shaking my hand as if we were about to begin a tennis match. He had two ribbons pinned to his left breast. I squeezed his hand harder than necessary. Richards had already begun to lay out his papers.

"I see you've got the National Defense Medal," I said. "Is that what you're doing here today? Defending the nation?" Blavitt's face went flat. "What's that other one for? Fire watch?"

Just then, three men in business suits came in and took seats at the back of the room away from the tables. I recognized one of them. "The company's sent some heavyweights," I said to Richards. "The guy in the middle is the director of marine personnel."

"Who are the other two?" he asked.

"I don't know."

A white-haired burly man came in and sat down at the table directly in front of us.

"Gentlemen, shall we begin?" he said. "I'm Judge Xavier R. Francis. This court is now in session." He banged the table with a small wooden gavel that looked like something one might find in a child's cooking set. "Will the defendant please rise? In the matter of Merchant Mariner's Document number Z-BK 185-36-0642, you are hereby charged to appear at this hearing under provisions of Revised Statute 4450, as amended, 46 United States Code 239, and the regulations promulgated thereunder, looking to the suspension or revocation of your merchant mariner's document. In the captioned matter, you are hereby charged with misconduct.

"First specification: In that you, while serving as wiper aboard a United States vessel under authority of the captioned documents, did, on 6 March 1974, while the vessel was at Long Beach, California, wrongfully have in your room aboard said vessel a Sucrets container which held seven cigarettes, each with a quantity of marijuana.

"Second specification: In that you, while serving as above, did, on 6 March 1974, while the vessel was at Long Beach, California, wrongfully have in your room aboard said vessel a plastic baggie which contained approximately ten grams of marijuana.

"Third specification: In that you, while serving as above, did, on 6 March 1974, while the vessel was at Long Beach, California, wrongfully have in your room aboard said vessel a silver-colored metal cigar tube which contained approximately one gram of marijuana.

"How do you plead?"

"Not guilty," I said.

"You may be seated," he said. "You have the right to be represented by professional counsel, or by any other person you may desire."

"I represent the defendant, your honor," said Richards, introducing himself.

"Let the record so indicate," said the judge. "You have the right to examine witnesses, and to cross-examine witnesses testifying against you. You have the right to introduce relevant evidence into the record, and object to documents introduced by the investigating officer. If you have witnesses to call, give me their names and addresses, and I'll have them subpoenaed. You may be sworn to testify, but cannot be compelled to testify. The burden of proof is on the investigating officer. Do you understand your rights?"

"I do," I said.

"Are there any motions to be considered at this time?"

"I have two motions, your honor," said Richards.

"Proceed, counsellor," said the judge.

"The first is a petition to dismiss the charges. My client never properly signed shipping articles as required by 46 USCA 564 in that the articles were never displayed or read to him. Furthermore, the alleged offenses with which my client is charged were never read to him by the ship's master, nor was he given the opportunity to make any reply thereto, and, in fact, my client believes and therefore avers that the charges were never even entered into the log book of the ship as required by 46 USCA 201 and 46 USCA 702. Thus no prosecution of these charges can be maintained against my client."

"Let me have that," said the judge. "And the second motion?"

"The second is a motion to suppress any evidence found in my client's stateroom on March 6th, 1974, or at any other time, for the following reasons: my client's stateroom on the date mentioned was searched, if it was searched at all, in my client's absence and in the absence of any search warrant and in the absence of my client's consent, which search warrant or consent to search is required, *inter alia*, by 18 USCA 2236."

"Let me see that one, too," said the judge.

"Your honor," said Richards, "I have additional evidence and several briefs to present in support of these motions."

"Should that be necessary, you'll have the oportunity to present further argument at the next session," said the judge. "Court will stand in recess until the morning of July 9th at ten a.m." He banged his little gavel, stood up, and walked out.

"That's it?" I said.

"That's it for today," said Richards.

"I've gotta wait another three weeks?"

"Delay is always to the advantage of the defense," said Richards.

*   *   *

"You were in the Marines, weren't you?" Ray Baker asked me the next day while we were stacking stockade fencing behind the warehouse.

"Yeh," I said.

"You got a tattoo."

"Yep."

"Did it hurt?"

"Not much."

"Were you drunk?"

"In a manner of speaking."

"What do you mean?" Ray said.

"Ask Daniel," I said. "He'll tell you."

"Daniel?" said Ray. "That Daniel?" He nodded his head in the direction of the showroom.

Daniel and I had gotten tattooed by Lyle Tuttle during a fast and furious trip to California at Christmas break of my sophomore year. We had been up all night driving from Laguna Beach to San Francisco, and while driving around trying to find Jack Gold's house, we'd gone right past Tuttle's studio.

"That guy tattooed Grace Slick," I'd said.

"Let's get tattoos," Daniel had said.

"Ask him about the scorpion on his right bicep," I told Ray, "Ask him about getting lost in the Twilight Zone."

Ray looked at me. He was just out of high school and the world was his for the taking, but he didn't quite know what to make of it. He tried not to let on. He drove a Harley-Davidson motorcycle and had a happy way about him. He was working parttime in the warehouse.

"I was thinking about joining the Marines," he said.

"You were?" I said.

"Yeh."

"What are you thinking about now?"

"Huh?" said Ray.

"It's a joke," I said.

"What is?"

"Never mind."

"What was it like?"

"What?"

"The Marines."

"They've got snappy uniforms, don't they?" I said. "Those dark blue ones with the gold piping and the sky blue trousers. You should definitely join the Marines if you want a sharp uniform."

"Did you have one like that?"

"Nope," I said. "Recruiters wear those. And embassy guards.

Spitshine jobs. I wore baggy green jungle utilities with mud all over them and three weeks of sweat."

"You serve in Nam?"

"Yep."

"Did you see a lot of action?"

"Depends on what you call a lot. Most of the time, nothing happened. But when something did happen, I wished I coulda been on another planet. Another planet, Ray. Someplace far away."

"Would you do it again?"

"Nope."

"You don't think I should join?"

"Nope."

"Why not?" he asked.

"You haven't been listening."

"I know a guy who joined last year," said Ray.

"Lots of guys join," I said. "I know a guy who joined the circus. He's a lion tamer. He climbs into a cage every day with a half-dozen lions. Why don't you join the circus?"

"You really think I shouldn't join?"

"Ray, what do you want, my benediction?"

"I just thought you might be able to give me a little advice."

"I did give you a little advice," I said. "You don't want advice. You want approval. I'm supposed to tell you it's okay for some asshole in the White House to send you halfway around the world to kill people you've never even met? I've done that. I didn't like it. You want to do it, I'm sure they'd love to have you."

Ritchie Lazzarri picked me up after work a few hours later. Ray was up in the loft sorting molding.

"Hey, Ray," I called up, "You think it's just me? Ask this guy." But Ray didn't want to talk. I left my car in the lot behind the warehouse, and we took Ritchie's car to Bethlehem to see some friends, old VVAW guys who'd been arrested with Ritchie a couple of times, back in the days of guerrilla theater.

Ritchie had been an aerial scout in Vietnam. His job had been to attract enemy fire, then direct air strikes and artillery and infantry onto whoever fired on him and his pilot. He had been shot down three times. Once his pilot had been killed in midair and he'd had to crashland the helicopter himself. Then he'd gone on R&R in Australia. It was the summer of 1968. He had watched the Chicago police riots at the Democratic National Convention in a luxury hotel in Sydney. He had stared and stared at the television set, watching the cops savagely beat anyone they could get their hands on: antiwar demonstrators, journalists, convention delegates, random passersby. He had tried to change the channel, but it was on all of them. When he got back to Vietnam, he had refused to fly another mission.

Two Silver Stars, two Bronze Stars, two Purple Hearts, and they had court martialed him. He had joined VVAW. He had returned his medals to Congress during Operation Dewey Canyon III in the spring of 1971, though his wife had threatened to divorce him if he did because she thought some day their sons might want them. His father had been forced off the Philadelphia Police Department after eighteen years because of Ritchie's vocal opposition to the war, though father and son had not spoken since the day Ritchie had come home from Vietnam.

"Why didn't you tell me it would be like that?" Ritchie had said to his father, a combat veteran of World War Two.

It was the first thing he had said. It was the only thing he had said. Then he had walked away. He had not gone home again. After several years of separation, he had reconciled with his wife, and they were living with their two young sons on a one-mule patch in West Virginia. They had a garden and a few animals, and he was a skilled carpenter. He'd come up alone for a visit.

"How's things with Kate?" I said.

"Okay," he said. "She's happier now that I'm not occupying the Statue of Liberty or getting arrested in Detroit."

"Does she understand why you did that stuff?"

"Not really. Don't look now, but there's a pigwagon behind us."

"Just be cool," I said. "Keep driving."

"His bubblegum machine is on."

84

"Ease over and let him pass," I said.

"I think he wants us."

"Terrific."

"I've got two ounces of hash taped to my ankle," he said.

"Oh, fucking terrific."

"Sorry. Butch wanted it."

We pulled over. The cop car pulled over behind us and two cops jumped out. Guns drawn, they stalked up to the car.

"Don't move," said the cop on Ritchie's side. He looked like Charleton Heston. Both cops had their revolvers pointed at our heads.

"What's the problem, man?" said Ritchie.

"One of your taillights is out," said Charleton Heston.

"You're going to shoot us because he's got a broken taillight?" I said.

"Out of the car nice and easy," said Charleton Heston. "Put your hands on the hood. Spread your feet. That's right." They patted us down one at a time. When Charleton Heston started down Ritchie's legs, I was puckered so hard I could barely keep my eyes open, but the cop missed the hash. Ritchie was wearing heavy leather boots. If they took us in and stripsearched us, they wouldn't miss it.

"Lemme see some identification," said Charleton Heston. "And you. Registration." He walked back to his car and got on the radio.

"Is this any way to treat a couple of vets who've shed their blood for that flag you're wearing?" Ritchie said to the younger cop.

"You guys Nam vets?" the cop asked.

"Yeh."

"Who were you with?"

"First of the Ninth, First Air Cav," said Ritchie.

"First Battalion, First Marines," I said.

"Hotel Two-Five," said the cop.

"Were you in Hue City?" I asked.

"Yeh," he said. "You?"

"That's where I got my Purple Heart," I said. "What are you treating us this way for? You oughta be ashamed of yourself."

"Hey, it's just routine."

"Guns drawn is routine?" I said. "For a broken taillight?"

Charleton Heston came back, made some personal remarks and threatening noises, and gave Ritchie a ticket for operating an unsafe motor vehicle. The young cop didn't say anything else. Ritchie shoved the ticket under his seat and we drove off.

"Coulda been worse," he said.

"You could have warned me," I said.

"Would it have mattered?"

"I guess not, but I've already got my ass in a sling. I could have had some time to be thinking about a plan. We could have eaten the stuff."

"Fuckin' pigs."

"That young guy was a Marine," I said. "Can you believe that?"

"After the revolution, baby."

"Ain't gonna be no revolution, Ritchie. Ain't nobody here but us chickens."

*   *   *

"He denied both motions?" I said. "Why?"

"He doesn't say," said Richards, holding the letter he had received from the judge. "'I'm satisfied that the proper ruling is to deny the application to suppress evidence and also your motion to dismiss the proceedings.' That's all he says."

"Is this what you call a hanging judge?"

"I know he thinks you're guilty."

"How do you know that?"

"I've been doing this for a long time."

"What do we do now?"

"Prepare a defense. How long was the relief crew on the ship?"

"They came on right after we docked. They were on board for at least twenty-four hours."

"And they had access to your room?"

"Well, yeh, they have access to the whole ship, but I had a key."

"Did you lock your door when you left the ship?"

"I don't remember."

"Who else had a key?"

"The first assistant engineer," I said. "Probably the chief engineer and the captain. Maybe some others, I don't know."

"Who was in your cabin before you occupied it?"

"The wiper I replaced. He injured his eye and had to get off the ship for treatment."

"Do you know what happened to his key?"

"No," I said. "He would have turned it in to the first engineer."

"But you don't know that he did that," Richards said.

"No."

"What did you do between the time the ship docked in Long Beach and the time of the raid?"

"I topped off the fresh water tanks," I said. "Then I went to my cabin, changed my clothes, and left the ship."

"This was Monday morning?"

"Yes. I took a taxi into town, rented a car, and drove down to Laguna Beach. I know a family that lives there. I stayed at the Barneslys' until the next afternoon, then I came back, turned in the car, and went back to the ship around five o'clock. I had dinner on board, then Roger the Engineer and I left the ship in his rental car about eight. We went to see his brother, who lives in Long Beach, then we went to three or four nightclubs and bars. After the bars closed, we drove over to Wilmington to try to find an afterhours club Roger had heard about, but we couldn't, so we went back to the ship about five or five-thirty a.m. I went straight to my cabin and went to bed. The next thing I know, there's Captain Ahab and his humorless minions."

"Can you verify all of this?" Richards asked.

"Sure. Mrs. Barnesly could vouch for me. And Roger could. And there's the sign-out book at the gate on the dock. You have to sign in and out to get through the gate."

87

"Who else had access to the ship?"

"The regular crew. And everybody who worked on the dock."

"Where was the alleged contraband when the search party found it?"

"You just can't bring yourself not to say 'alleged,' can you?"

"The burden of proof is on the government," Richards said. "You're innocent until proven guilty. And they're the ones who've got to prove it. That's not my job."

"They can do a lot of damage to innocent people without finding them guilty in a court of law. You ever hear of the Gainesville Eight?"

"Not now."

"Seven of them were honorably discharged Vietnam veterans. Bronze Stars, Purple Hearts, Cross of Gallantry—"

"Not now," he said. "Where was the alleged contraband when the search party found it?"

"On my desk."

"Out in the open?"

"I think the joints were. The other stuff wasn't."

"Where was it?"

"I don't remember exactly. There were some little drawers, and some little cubbies like you'd find on an old-fashioned roll-top desk. It was stashed in there somewhere."

"Did the search party knock on your door?"

"If they did, I didn't hear it."

"Did anyone ask your permission to come in?"

"Not that I heard."

"You didn't give your permission for them to come in?"

"No. I opened my eyes and there they were."

"What did they say to you?"

"The captain told me to get dressed," I said. "Then he told me to wait in the passageway. Then he told me to come back in. They showed me what they'd found, tossed it all into a big envelope, and made a big show of sealing it in my presence. I think the envelope had my name on it, and the date and time. Then the captain told me not to leave the cabin, and they left."

"They didn't say anything else?"

"No."

"They didn't ask you if the alleged contraband was yours?"

"No."

"Did you say anything to any of them?"

"Out in the hall, I asked the bosun for a cigarette, but he wouldn't give me one."

"You didn't say anything else?"

"No. I was scared shitless, but I knew enough to keep my mouth shut. What are you thinking?"

"I'm thinking we may be able to raise the possibility that somebody else could have entered your cabin in your absence. You didn't spend much time on the ship for most of the two days before the raid, but a lot of other people did. All we need to establish is reasonable doubt."

"With this judge?"

"He's subject to appeal," Richards said, "And he knows it. He can't rule on his feelings alone."

"Look at this," I said. I'd been leafing through *The Law of Seamen*, which had been sitting on Richards's desk. " 'Section 100. The articles also provide that no dangerous weapons or grog are allowed on the vessel or are to be brought on her.' Practically every man on the ship was in violation of that one all the time, the captain included. Everybody drank. Nobody even attempted to hide it. Some of the men were hardcore alcoholics."

"Be that as it may, unfortunately the moral terpitude of the rest of the ship's complement isn't on trial here."

"No, they want the witch, don't they?"

"Witches are female. You would be a warlock."

"Whatever. Maybe we could use the Colson defense." Charles Colson had been Nixon's hatchetman, but he claimed to have had a religious conversion subsequent to his indictment. He'd copped a plea and received a light sentence. "I could say the president ordered me to do it, and bring my prayer group to court with me."

"Did you see this?" Richards asked. It was an article about the dangers of marijuana. Quoting the *New England Journal of Medicine*, the article said that regular marijuana use caused lowered sperm count and sexual impotence in men.

"I don't know about the lowered sperm count," I said, "but I'm not sexually impotent. And with a lowered sperm count, I would think it's harder to cause an accidental pregnancy. Seems to me, it's a godsend. They've been trying to prove that pot's bad for you ever since the repeal of prohibition, and they haven't done it yet. They did a study in California a few years ago where they 'proved' marijuana causes mental disorientation and physical impairment. They forced a bunch of rabbits to smoke about a freight car full of pot in about six hours. They've even got a smoking machine they strap the rabbits to so they have to inhale smoke every time they breathe. It's a wonder the rabbits were still in this galaxy. I couldn't smoke that much dope in a lifetime. How'd you like to be the scientist who cooks up experiments like that? Is that sick?"

"I thought you'd find it interesting," he said. "Lieutenant Blavitt gave me his witness list."

"Lieutenant junior grade," I said. "He's only a j.g."

"Whatever. He's going to call Captain Kyle and a Special Agent Leaderman."

"I wonder if he's the guy in the search party I'd never seen before."

"Must be," said Richards. "He's in charge of corporate security for the oil company. I wonder how long the company held the evidence before they turned it over to the Coast Guard."

"Does it matter?"

"It could. My guess is they've got even less experience handling criminal evidence than the Coast Guard does. And the longer the chain of custody, the more chances there are for mistakes. Have you thought any more about law school?"

"Not much."

"I think you should."

"I know you do."

"I got my degree from George Washington Law School," he said. "I've been a very active alumnus. A recommendation from me might carry some weight. You've got a good academic record, don't you?"

"Yes."

"How good?"

"Three point seven," I said.

"Very good indeed. All you'd have to do is take the law boards. Why don't you find out when they're given, and write to GW for a catalog and application?"

"Can you imagine me as a lawyer?"

"As a matter of fact, I can," he said.

"I'll think about it," I said.

"You do that."

*   *   *

I tried to get my mother to ride in the MG, but she wouldn't. "If you ever managed to get me into that," she said, pointing at the car and laughing, "you'd never get me out again." She was middle-aged and overweight, and it was very small. I did get my father to ride in it once, but he held onto the dashboard as if he were riding the Wild Mouse at Dorney Park. I imagined him imagining himself about to die like a bug beneath the wheels of a screaming semi. He didn't say three words during the entire ride, which was just as well because when he did talk, all he had to tell me was who he'd buried, baptized, or married since the last time I'd seen him.

While I was in Vietnam, my father had preached a sermon about the war. "I'm tired of being on the defensive over Vietnam," he had said. "I suspect the real motives of the hecklers and hippies are selfish and self-serving. Could it just not be possible there are still those who feel an obligation to our country if one wants all the privileges and benefits? It just might also be that the heroism of our brave soldiers may pass in somber review long after the embittered nonsense of our day has become a shabby footnote to a time we shall wish to forget."

The sermon was a big hit. The Perkasie *News-Herald* did an article about my father and his sermon. The article was picked up by the Allentown *Morning Call*, and read into the *Congressional Record* by the Honorable Frederick B. Rooney of Pennsylvania, U.S. House of Representatives.

"What kind of heroism were you thinking of, Pop?" I had asked him after I'd joined the ranks of the hecklers and hippies, "Like when we gang-banged that girl in Hue City?" Such discussions usually lasted eight or ten seconds before my mother would have to send us to neutral corners. After awhile, I stopped baiting him.

Like most of his generation, he saw the behavior of my generation as an attack on everything he believed in, which it was. Unlike most of the men in his generation, he had played no part in the Second World War. Just out of divinity school, he had tried to become a navy chaplain, but he'd flunked the physical. The army would have taken him if he had pressed for a waiver of the physical requirements, but for reasons he never shared, he had not pressed for a waiver.

Instead, he had spent his war in Cashtown, Pennsylvania, preaching God's love and victory over the Japs and the Jerries. Then, only three weeks before the Nazi surrender, his first cousin, who had been his closest childhood companion, stepped on a landmine in Germany and was dismembered for his trouble. My father would spend the rest of his life believing that Cousin Bob had died because of my father's cowardice. Convinced that he'd missed his chance at manhood, he couldn't fathom a son who wished that he had never been on the same planet as a war zone. After awhile, I had given up trying to explain. We did okay if I stuck to sports and the weather.

I pulled into the driveway behind the parsonage and helped my father pry his fingers out of the dashboard. He disappeared into the church office next door to thank God for his deliverance from eighteen-wheelers. My mother was weeding the garden I'd made for her.

"Robert Richards wants me to go to law school," I told her. "He's offered to write a recommendation for me."

"You shouldn't let an offer like that go to waste," she said, leaning on her hoe. I could see a glimmer of hope rising in her eyes, as if her wayward son might amount to something after all.

"Seems a little strange to be contemplating a career at law while I'm standing before the bar trying to stay out of jail."

"Well, you're certainly getting an insider's perspective on it," she said.

"You've got a great sense of humor, Mom."

"Would you like to be a lawyer?"

"Nixon's a lawyer," I said.

"So is Mister Richards," she said.

"I don't know. I guess I really can't drive a forklift for the rest of my life."

"Your father always wanted one of you boys to follow him into the ministry," she said.

"When our guys got killed, the chaplain used to say it was God's will, but when the gooks got killed, he said it was God's wrath. You figure it out. He used to carry a loaded rifle with a little sign taped to the stock that said, 'The Chaplain's Assistant.' God must have liked that a lot, don't you think?"

"I think it would be nice if you went to law school," she said. "Pull up that weed there, over by the zinneas."

*   *   *

"Your honor," Richards began, "I was under the impression that I would have the chance to present additional evidence and briefs in support of these motions."

"If it became necessary," said the judge. "It won't be necessary. On your motion to dismiss, I am satisfied that imperfectly executed articles are not grounds for dismissal. Neither are procedural irregularities concerning the ship's log. On your petition to suppress, the master has the absolute right to search any part of his vessel for contraband. The crew ships at the master's convenience. The Fourth Amendment does not apply."

"For the record, your honor, I would like to enter an objection to each of your denials."

"So noted," said the judge. "Is the government ready to present its case?"

Blavitt went through a boilerplate synopsis of the charges, and entered for identification a certified copy of the shipping articles and my discharge certificate. He stated that Lieutenant (j.g.) Thomas Purcell had received a sealed envelope from Special Agent Leaderman on April 5th, 1974, and placed it into a Coast Guard vault in Long Beach the same day. He submitted a chain of custody document detailing where the envelope had gone from that day. Then he offered a Sucrets container, a baggie, a cigar tube, and a lab analysis from the University of California at Los Angeles medical school lab. The oil company's director of marine personnel and his two companions were again sitting at the back of the room.

The first witness Blavitt called was Henry Kyle. As Kyle entered the room, dressed in a dark blue suit that didn't seem to belong to him, he walked with the suggestion of a stoop. His face was drawn and his skin translucent. He had retired since I'd last seen him. Without a ship to command, Kyle seemed diminished. He took the oath and identified himself, then Blavitt asked him if he could identify me.

"I recognize him," said Kyle.

"Let the record show that the witness is pointing to the defendant," said the judge.

"He was the wiper," said Kyle.

"Objection," said Richards, "That hasn't been established yet."

"Overruled."

"Is this the agreement between you and the defendant, commonly known as the ship's articles?" Blavitt asked.

94

"Yes, it is."

"How did the defendant's name come to be on this?"

"He signed it when he came aboard."

Blavitt then offered my discharge certificate for Kyle's identification before proceeding.

"Did you order and conduct a search of your vessel on March 6th, 1974?"

"I did."

"Why?"

"I had reason to believe there were numerous amounts of narcotics on the vessel," Kyle said.

"And what caused you to believe this?" asked Blavitt.

"There had been a general disregard for duty among a number of the ship's crew."

"What did you find in the defendant's room?"

"We found some marijuana cigarettes, about ten or twelve."

"These?" said Blavitt, taking several out of the Sucrets container.

"They appear to be the ones."

Kyle identified the baggy and the cigar tube as well, then Richards began his cross-examination.

"You say you found ten or twelve marijuana cigarettes in my client's room, but he's only charged with having seven cigarettes. What happened to the other three? Or was it five?"

"I don't recall the exact number. They were all in that box."

"Where in my client's room were the items in question found?"

"They were on his desk."

"Could you explain where exactly?"

"Everybody witnessed that they were on his desk."

"But where on his desk?" Richards asked.

"I can't recall exactly," said Kyle, "Where it was, was right on his desk."

"How did you know that what you found was marijuana?"

"Well, it looked like marijuana. It smelled like it."

"Are you a chemist?"

"Well, no, but—"

"Then you didn't know what you had found, did you?"

"We had reason to believe it was marijuana."

"But you don't know that for a fact, do you?"

"No."

"Did you ask my client anything during your search?"

"I asked him if he was under medical care, and he said no, positively not."

"What did you do with what you found?"

"I turned it over to our corporate security officer, Bob Leaderman."

"You said you had reason to believe there were narcotics aboard because a number of the crew exhibited a general disregard for their duty. Was my client among that number?"

"I don't recall."

"You don't recall?"

"He could have been. I don't recall specifically."

"Your engineering officers thought he was an exemplary seaman," Richards said. "'Dependable.' 'Responsible.' 'Eager to learn.' 'Capable.' You must have concurred with their assessment. You transferred my client from the steward's department to the engine department on the basis of these recommendations. You even had to waive your company's six-month rule to do it. You don't recall any of this?"

"Objection, your honor," said Blavitt. "The defendant's character and past performance are not at issue here."

"But your honor," said Richards, "It goes to probable cause, or the lack thereof."

"The master doesn't need probable cause," said the judge. "It is his duty to search for contraband. Objection sustained."

"Where was the defendant when you entered his stateroom?" Richards asked.

"He appeared to be asleep," Kyle said. "He was lying in his berth when I walked in. I had the whole party with me. He was definitely nude from the waist down. His hair was all, it was long

96

and wild, all tangled. You could hardly tell him for a human being."

"How long was the relief crew on board during the time the ship was in Long Beach?"

"I don't recall exactly. The relief crew was aboard when it was searched. There could have been a previous relief."

"Was it the policy that the wiper would be off when the relief crew was aboard?"

"The whole crew was off," said Kyle.

"Did the dock crew have access to the ship?"

"Only to the working areas."

"Were the doors leading to the crew's quarters kept locked?"

"Well, no."

"So anyone aboard the ship could have had access to my client's stateroom?"

"Well, yes, theoretically."

"Theoretically. This copy of the ship's articles," said Richards. "Is that your signature?" Kyle studied it intently for a few seconds.

"Well, no, I believe that is Mr. James's signature, my radio officer."

"But it says Henry Kyle, Master of the Vessel."

"He often took care of my routine paperwork. I authorized him to do so."

"My client's name is typed onto this list," said Richards. "He hasn't signed these articles. Anyone could have typed his name here."

"He would have signed the continuation of the articles aboard the ship," Kyle said. "This master list was prepared by the company office at my direction. I submitted his name to them."

"What is this continuation of articles you referred to?"

"It's a running list of new crew members."

"Does it include the text of the articles?"

"Well, no, but copies are posted on the fo'csle card and elsewhere about the ship."

"But you didn't read them to my client or offer him a chance to read them prior to his alleged signing?"

"Objection, your honor."

"Sustained."

"But your honor, there's been no evidence presented to indicate that my client actually signed the articles."

"I've already ruled on the relevance of that. Please proceed."

"Is this your signature?" Richards asked, offering my discharge certificate to Kyle.

"No, that again is Mr. James's signature."

"But it says Henry Kyle, Master of the Vessel."

"Objection. We've already established that the captain authorized the radio officer to sign for him."

"Your honor," said Richards, "the witness stated that his radio officer was authorized to handle routine paperwork. I would submit that the summary discharge of a seaman for an alleged offense carrying criminal liability is hardly routine."

"Regardless of the reason," said Blavitt, "signing of the discharge certificate is a routine duty. It's done whenever a seaman leaves a vessel for whatever reason."

"Objection sustained."

"Were you present when my client was discharged from the ship?"

"Yes, I believe I was."

"But you had your radio officer sign the certificate anyway?"

"Yes."

"Why didn't you sign it yourself?"

"I don't recall."

"You don't recall?"

"No."

"No further questions, your honor."

"He's lying," I said as soon as Richards sat down. "He wasn't there when I got booted. And he never asked me if I was under medical care."

"We'll take a brief recess before the next witness," said the judge. As I stood up to stretch my legs, Kyle walked over to me.

"Well, I guess I can shake your hand," he said, extending his.

"You just swore under oath that you could hardly tell me for a human being," I said, "and now you guess you can shake my hand?! Well, I guess not." Richards spread a hand over my shoulder, dug his fingers in hard, and turned me away from Kyle. "Did you hear what he said about me?" I said.

"Yes," said Richards. "And the judge did, too. I would rather the judge ponder the captain's outburst than yours."

When the judge reconvened, Blavitt called Leaderman to the stand. "What were your duties?" he asked.

"To investigate all thefts and acts of sabotage against the company and its property," Leaderman said.

"Did you search the defendant's stateroom on March 6th?"

"I did. I was with Captain Kyle and several others," he said, naming them.

"What did you find?"

"We found several handrolled cigarettes—they appeared to be marijuana—in a small tin box, and also a baggie and a metal cigar tube containing what appeared to be marijuana."

"Is this what you found?"

"Yes. You can see my initials on the cigarettes. Right there. REL."

"And these other items?"

"Yes, they appear to be the same ones we found."

"Your honor, I request that exhibits four, five, and six be entered into evidence."

"Objection, your honor," said Richards. "Exhibits five and six are not initialed. You can buy baggies at any supermarket, and cigar tubes at any tobacco shop. There's no way the witness can positively identify these as the ones he found."

"I'll admit exhibit four," said the judge. "For the time being, I'll sustain the rest of your objection."

"What did you do with the contraband you found?" said Blavitt.

"Objection, your honor. The fact that contraband was found has not yet been established. The witness testified that the substance appeared to be marijuana, but he's not qualified to state that for a fact."

"Sustained."

"What did you do with the items you found in the defendant's room?" said Blavitt.

"I put it all into a large envelope. Everyone present signed the envelope, then I put it into the company's security vault at my office."

"Is this the envelope?"

"Yes, that's it."

"No further questions, your honor."

"Cross-examination?" said the judge.

"Mister Leaderman," said Richards, "was my client suspected of theft or sabotage?"

"No."

"But you said your duty is to investigate theft or sabotage."

"I handle other matters as well, anything involving security."

"I see. What instructions did you give to the other members of the search party?"

"I told them that if they found anything that looked like contraband, they should call it to my attention immediately."

"Were you the one who found these items?"

"I, no, I believe it was Mister Davis."

"And he is?"

"He's the company's union chairman."

"And he brought them to your attention?"

"Yes."

"Where were you at the time?"

"In the defendant's room."

"Where in the room?"

"I don't recall exactly. Looking through a wall locker, I think."

"So you didn't actually see Mister Davis find these items?"

"Well, no, but I was right there in the room with him."

"But you don't know where he found them, or when he found them."

"He found them during the search. They were on the defendant's desk."

"They were on the defendant's desk when you saw them, but

where were they when Mister Davis found them?"

"He said he found them on the desk."

"Isn't it possible that Mister Davis could have brought these items into my client's room with him and placed them on the desk himself?"

"I've known Fred Davis for fourteen years—"

"I'm not asking you about your relationship with Mister Davis," said Richards. "Isn't it possible he could have placed these items on my client's desk himself?"

"Well, yes, theoretically, I suppose it's possible, but—"

"Or another member of the search party?"

"Theoretically, yes," said Leaderman.

"Theoretically yes," said Richards. "Where was my client when you entered his room?"

"I don't recall. I believe he was sleeping."

"At any time after you entered the room, did my client ever go anywhere near his desk?"

"I don't recall. I don't believe so."

"Did you say anything to my client before, during, or after the search?"

"When it was completed, we asked him, Captain Kyle asked him if he was under medical supervision. He said no."

"When did you put the envelope in the company safe?"

"On March 7th."

"Where was the evidence between March 6th and March 7th?"

"I put it in the trunk of my car and locked it."

"You left it in the trunk of your car?"

"Yes. No one else has a key but me."

"Do you own the car?"

"It's a company car."

"And there is only one set of keys for it?"

"To the best of my knowledge. I'm the only one who uses it."

"Only one set of keys for a company car?"

"Objection, your honor," said Blavitt. "The witness has already responded."

"Sustained. Proceed, counsellor," said the judge.

"And you turned the envelope over to the Coast Guard on April 5th?"

"Yes."

"Was it in the company safe for the entire time between March 7th and April 5th?"

"Yes."

"Who had access to that safe?"

"Only myself and two, three other people."

"So three other people besides yourself had access to the envelope during a period of over four weeks."

"The envelope was sealed. I delivered it to the Coast Guard with the seal intact."

"How was it sealed?"

"With Scotch tape. Everyone in the party signed the envelope across the flap, and then I sealed it with Scotch tape."

"Scotch tape?"

"Yes."

"What about this notation? 'J.2 4/17/74.' It appears to be under the Scotch tape."

"I wouldn't know about that," said Leaderman. "I turned it over to the Coast Guard on April 5th. The seal was intact at that time."

"You said that everyone signed the envelope, but the envelope is signed only by you and Captain Kyle. Are you sure this is the envelope into which you put the items you found in my client's stateroom?"

"Well, yes. I guess the captain and I signed it, but the others witnessed it."

"I see. Twice you've said that everyone in the search party signed the envelope, but now you guess that only you and the captain signed it. No further questions, your honor."

Then Blavitt asked that the UCLA lab report be admitted into evidence.

"Objection, your honor," said Richards. "This lab report has nothing to do with my client. It mentions four gray envelopes

102

containing marijuana without identifying any envelope as belonging to a particular crew member. The report contains the names of two seamen, neither of which is my client. In fact, nowhere in this report is my client's name mentioned. Moreover, it gives the total weight of the marijuana in all four envelopes, but does not say how much was in each individual envelope. Nor does it mention seven marijuana cigarettes, nor ten grams nor one gram, the amounts with which my client is charged with having in his possession. Nor does it mention a Sucrets container, a baggie, or a cigar tube. In addition, the report states that this material was delivered to the lab by the U.S. Marines. What were the U.S. Marines doing with this material? My client is a former Marine, your honor, a highly decorated combat veteran, but he was honorably discharged in 1969. The U.S. Marines have nothing to do with my client or this case, and this lab report appears to have nothing to do with my client or the U.S. Coast Guard."

"Objection sustained," said the judge.

"May I have a brief recess, your honor?" said Blavitt, who did not look well.

"Court stands in recess," said the judge. Blavitt went into a huddle with Jeffries.

"I think we've got them," Richards said.

"Wouldn't that be nice?" I said.

"Wouldn't it? Did you notice the way I slipped your military service into the record?"

"Highly decorated?" I said.

"You've got more decorations than they do," said Richards, nodding toward Blavitt and Jeffries.

I went out into the hall to have a cigarette. The director of marine personnel and his two pals were already there. They turned and glared at me for a long moment before turning away.

"Your honor," Blavitt began a few minutes later, "I request permission to submit these items to the Philadelphia Police Department's crime lab for further analysis. I believe we can correct the deficiencies in the original report."

"Objection, your honor. The chain of custody has not yet been established. These materials could have come from anywhere."

"I'm going to overrule your objection, counsellor," said the judge. "In the interest of expediting these proceedings, I'm going to grant permission for this request. The chemist who performs the analysis is to be available to testify at this hearing when it reconvenes at ten a.m. on August 12th. Until then, this court stands in recess."

"How the hell can he do that?!" I said to Richards.

"Be quiet," said Richards. "Let's go." We went to the coffeeshop across the street from the customs building.

"For chrissake, Robert, this is justice? How can the judge do that? How the hell can he do that?"

"I'm not sure what he's up to yet, but I'll find out before August 12th."

"Another month I've got to wait?"

"Delay is always—"

"Not this time. No. They've got a fucked up lab report, so they can just go out and get another one? This guy's out to hang me, that's what he's up to."

"We'll see," said Richards.

"You're worried, aren't you?"

"I'm always worried until I hear the verdict. That's my job. It's not yours."

"Easy enough for you to say."

"We're not licked yet. Have you written to GW?"

"Just at the moment, I'm not too enamored of your profession."

"You will be. Have you written to them?"

"Yes."

"We might make something of you yet."

*　　*　　*

That Friday night, I took off to visit Ritchie Lazzarri in West Virginia. I got off work at nine, and left directly from Panel Emporium because it was a seven-hour drive each way and I had to be

104

back by Monday morning. It had been a hot day, and even after sunset the air was warm enough to leave the top down. I liked driving at night, especially late at night when there were few other cars on the road. I could turn off my headlights and run on the parking lights alone. They gave just enough illumination to follow the road while leaving my night vision intact so that I could see the surrounding countryside. In Vietnam, I had learned how to read the night landscape by using my peripheral vision and never allowing my eyes to stare directly at one point the way you would in the daytime, and it was exhilarating to barrel along at sixty miles an hour in near-total darkness. With the top down, I could look up at the stars and imagine myself among them.

I had found the Big Dipper and was looking for the Pole Star when I suddenly realized with a skip of the heart that I wasn't alone. It should have scared the bejesus out of me, but by now I was getting used to it.

"I thought I told you guys to knock," I said.

"We sent you a letter," said Ski. "Didn't you get it?"

Bobby was sitting in the right front seat. There weren't any back seats, but Frenchie and Ski were wedged in between the seats and the back wall of the tiny trunk, their knees scrunched up against their chests, their feet and legs intertwined because they were sitting kind of sideways.

"Nobody can ride like that," I said.

"We don't mind," said Ski.

"Nice car," said Frenchie. "This is fun."

"I'll get a ticket if I get spotted with four people in this car."

"You'll get a ticket if you get spotted driving without your head-lights," said Ski.

"Don't sweat it," said Frenchie. "Who's gonna see us?"

"Why me?" I said.

"Just lucky, I guess," said Ski.

"No, really, why me?"

"How should we know?" said Frenchie. "We're angels, not psy-chiatrists."

"Am I the only one you guys do this to? What about Mogerdy? What about Seagrave?"

"Everybody that was there can see us," said Ski. "Or guys like us. But they don't all see the same thing. Most of 'em don't know what they're seeing. Some guys cry in their sleep. Some guys get all choked up when they hear the Star Spangled Banana. Some guys hear voices, but they turn around and nobody's there. Everybody's different."

"Oh," I said.

"So how's it going?" said Ski.

"Did you hear what happened the other day?"

"About that lab report?" he said.

"Yeh."

"We heard."

"Where were you last week?"

"Where we always are," said Ski. "We miss something?"

"I got hassled by the pigs again," I said. "One of 'em turned out to be a Jarhead from the Fifth Marines."

"The man ought to be ashamed of himself," said Ski.

"That's what I told him," I said. "That's exactly what I told him. I'm getting really tired of people with badges sticking guns in my face."

"I know what you mean," said Ski.

"I'll bet you do," I said.

"You sure you don't want us to look up Tricky Dick for ya?" said Frenchie.

"I'd like to pay a visit to ol' LBJ down there on the Pedernales," said Ski.

"He's dead," I said.

"Son of a bitch," he said.

"And what about the rest of 'em?" I said. "What about the Rusks and the Rostows and the McNamaras and the Bundys? Henry the K. Melvin the Laird. Hell, Harry Truman, Dean Acheson, John Foster Dulles. What about all those generals? Maxwell Taylor. William Waste More Land. Cretin Abrams."

106

"I see what you mean," said Ski.

"What about the folks who think we shoulda sent the demonstrators UPS to the bottom of Lake Erie and nuked Hanoi while we had the chance?"

"If parents really loved their children," said Bobby, "there wouldn't be any wars." It was the first time Bobby had spoken. He'd been riding along with his head laid back on the headrest, just staring up at the stars.

"He's okay," said Frenchie, flipping his thumb in Bobby's direction. "Just got a little bad news, that's all."

"What happened?"

"My wife got married."

"I should hope so," I said.

"To another man," said Bobby.

"Oh."

Bobby and the girl he'd married had grown up together. They had dated all through high school and gotten married three weeks before he'd left for Vietnam.

"Give the girl a break," said Frenchie. "You been dead for seven years."

"My old sweetheart's got three kids already," said Ski. "She used to keep my picture on the table beside her bed, but she put it away when she started dating again."

"I'm sorry about your wife," I said. "Really. But Frenchie's right."

"I know," Bobby said. "I'll get used to it, I guess. Whatever happened to that cute little blonde you were going to marry?"

"She sent me a Dear John letter about four months after you bought the farm," I said.

"I didn't buy the farm," said Bobby. "I lost the farm. I grew up on a farm. It would have been mine some day."

"What blonde?" said Ski.

"She was gone by the time you showed up," I said.

"He used to keep a picture of her hanging in the hooch," said Bobby. "I still remember that picture. She was wearing a blue sweater that

107

matched her eyes. And a string of pearls. What happened?"

"It was a high school romance, that's all," I said. "Wouldn't have lasted two months if I'd gone to college. I was scared and I needed something to hold onto, so I made Jenny into my own personal Virgin Mary, but she was just a seventeen-year-old with no one to take her to the prom. She got tired of sitting home alone. There wasn't much between us but hormones. I invented the rest."

"I was gonna get married when I got home," said Ski. "I was gonna have a big parade and let everybody buy me drinks and then get married. I was gonna buy a big car and never have to walk anywhere again."

"You wanna drive for awhile?" I said.

"I can't," he said. "My driver's license expired."

"So did you," said Frenchie. Then he guffawed loudly.

"You're a scream," said Ski.

"What the hell," said Frenchie, "nobody lives forever."

"I would have settled for another thirty or forty years," said Bobby.

"I would have settled for one more good fuck," said Ski.

I'd always envied Ski because he was from California, a place that had acquired mythical proportions after the summer I'd spent there with Pete Konrad. The girls wore real bikinis, not the old-fashioned two-piece bathing suits that were still the style in Ocean City, New Jersey, back when I'd been in high school. Ski had shot the pier at Huntington Beach on his surfboard, and he'd had enough facial hair to grow a moustache. Once during an operation up near the DMZ, I hadn't shaved for three weeks, but all I'd had to show for it was a fuzzy little patch that nobody else could see.

The day Ski had gotten hit, I'd lent him my flak jacket to go check the mail. You weren't supposed to leave the bunkers at Con Thien without one, so when the cries of "Corpsman!" went up after a barrage of North Vietnamese artillery went off nearby, I had not been able to help with the wounded. Only later had I found out that Seagrave, Walters, and Stemkowski had been hit and choppered out. Seagrave and Walters had come back after a month in a hospital near Da Nang. Ski hadn't survived the medevac. Neither had my flak jacket.

"How come you ain't married yet?" said Frenchie.

"I don't even have a girlfriend."

"How come?" he said.

"I had a steady girlfriend for awhile in college, but I beat her up after King Richard the Milhous invaded Cambodia, so she dumped me. Can't imagine why, can you?"

"Why'd you do that?" said Bobby.

"Damned if I know," I said. "You guys don't know what it's like."

"We hear things," said Ski.

"But you didn't come back," I said. "You never had to look the beast right in the eye and realize you were it. Bear any burden, pay any price. It was all just fairy tales."

"We know that stuff," said Frenchie. "We told ya, we hear things."

"But you don't have to live with it," I said. "Christ, that jackass Nixon jerking off at the mouth about Peace With Honor, and all I can think of is that woman down on Go Noi Island with her chest ripped open and a dead baby in her arms. We've been doing shit like that since the Pilgrims stepped off the boat. It just goes on and on. We were part of something evil, guys. I still am."

"Don't be so hard on yourself," said Bobby. "It wasn't your fault."

"What difference does that make?" I said. "Who pulled the trigger?"

"Listen to me," he said. "Don't be so hard on yourself."

"Sometimes I feel like it's all coming straight down on me and there's nowhere to run and nowhere to hide and no pot to piss in. It's been like that ever since I came back. Everything hurts inside."

"I know what you mean," said Ski.

"He does," said Bobby. "So do I. But you've got to remember something."

"What?" I said.

"You're better off than we are," he said.

"Well, yes, there is that," I said. "But it doesn't feel that way sometimes." I could see the glow of headlights from an oncoming car that was still below the horizon of a rise in the road ahead of me. I was going to tell Bobby that being lost in America wasn't much better than being dead, but I knew that wasn't true, and anyway, by the time I'd switched on my headlights, they were gone. Nearly three a.m. An hour to go, more or less.

*   *   *

An hour later, I found myself on a narrow unpaved lane as rugged as the sand tracks through the Pine Barrens. Then it got worse. When I started encountering ruts and washouts big enough to swallow the MG, I began to wonder if I had goofed up Ritchie's directions. If I got stuck out here, I'd be stuck until daybreak with the nearest help likely to be some redneck hillbilly with a loaded shotgun and a distaste for long hair.

Once in Montana, three years earlier, I had stopped at a rickety general store to buy some beer. I went to the cash register to pay for it, but the middle-aged man behind the counter didn't look up from the newspaper he was reading.

"Excuse me," I had said, "I'd like to pay for this." He didn't respond for awhile, then he lowered the paper and peered over the top of it, his expression blank and flat as a dinnerplate.

"We don't sell nothin' to hippies," he had said. Three other men emerged from a room at the back of the store. They were all twice my age, three times my size, and built like cattle.

"Oh," I had said. "Then I'll just put this back and go."

Further down the road, I had tried again at a gas station, but the two attendants started throwing rocks at my car before I shut off the engine, which was just as well because I was in a hurry to leave there, too.

It took me thirty minutes to nurse the MG half a mile. When I got to Ritchie's place, he was standing on the front porch. "I heard you coming," he said.

110

"A bit off the beaten path, aren't you?" I said.

"That's the idea," he said. "How was the drive?"

"Fine."

"No pigs?"

"Not this time," I said. "I had some company, though."

"Pick up a hitchhiker?"

"Not exactly," I said. "Ritchie, do you ever see guys you used to know in Vietnam?"

"Once or twice," he said. "No, three times. Why?"

"I mean dead guys."

"Nightmares? Yeh, I still have nightmares."

"I don't mean nightmares," I said. "I had three guys in the car tonight. Guys I used to know in Vietnam. They all died there."

"Are you all right?"

"I'm fine, I think, but I turn around and there they are. This isn't the first time, either. They talk to me. They just hang around and we talk like we're talking now."

"Three of them?"

"Yeh."

"In that car?"

"Yeh."

"Have you been dropping acid lately?"

"No," I said. "They're real. They're not real, but they are. Bobby touched my cheek one time. He reached out his hand and touched me with his fingertips. They were warm. Do you think I'm crazy?"

"Do I think you're crazy?" he said.

"Yes," I said.

"That time my pilot got killed, we were up about two thousand feet and we banked left and he took a round right through his head and there I was, wearing his brains. I don't know how I got that chopper down. Somebody was talking to me. Somebody told me what to do and I did it. Rough landing, but I did it."

"But you'd been flying enough that you probably knew, ya know, subconsciously, what to do."

"Maybe," he said. "But somebody was talking to me. It wasn't

111

my voice. 'Do this, do that, now do this other thing.' I should be dead, but I'm not. I like ghosts."

"So do I," I said. "That's the weird part. I enjoy these guys. It's like they're not dead when they're with me."

"Maybe that's why they hang around," he said, gesturing up at the stars. "Big universe out there. Who knows what the hell goes on? If I were you, I wouldn't worry about it. You're just a normal dude having a normal extrasensory experience. What's to worry about?"

I rolled my sleepingbag out on the porch and went to sleep. In the morning, I awoke to the smell of fresh coffee and blueberry pancakes. I washed up at the pump behind the house, one of those old-fashioned pumps with a long handle you push up and down. The house looked sturdy, but very plain, just a one-story wooden box on cinderblocks with an unrailed porch across the front and a smaller covered porch in back.

Nearby was a small shed that doubled as a garage for Ritchie's car and a barn for the two goats and a dozen chickens. Beyond the outhouse was a large garden: corn, tomatoes, squash, peas, beans, peppers, several marijuana plants, cucumbers, all sorts of stuff. The whole place sat at the head of a steep valley divided among pastures, cornfields, and woods. I could see cows in several of the pastures, but the cows weren't Ritchie's. No other house was visible.

Inside was a partially closed-off kitchen with a wood-burning stove and a sink fed by a smaller handpump, and a combination living room–dining room with another wood stove and a sofa that doubled as Kate and Ritchie's bed. The boys, Jonathan and David, slept in a corner loft Ritchie had built. There was no plumbing, but they had electricity. Ritchie was making pancakes and Kate was giving David a bath at the sink.

"What do you do about the driveway when it snows?" I said.

"Nothing," said Ritchie. "We don't travel much in the winter anyway. When Jonathan starts school, maybe I'll get a tractor. Maybe not. We've been thinking about teaching the boys ourselves.

112

I'm not too keen on having them say the Pledge of Allegiance every day."

"How do you get along around here?"

"Oh, we've got everything we need," he said. "We grow most of what we eat, and what we can't grow I can barter for. I do carpentry."

"I don't mean that," I said. "How do you get along with your neighbors? Where the hell are your neighbors?"

"Down the road a piece," he said. "Town's over that way. It was a little strange when we first got here, but I'm a good carpenter and people respect that. I give 'em a decent day's work, and we don't talk much about politics or religion."

Later Ritchie introduced me to what he called "my favorite sport: porch-settin'." He had made two beautiful rockers, and from the front porch you could look down the whole length of the valley.

"You pay that ticket?" I said.

"Westmoreland ate it," he said. "I fixed the taillight, though." Westmoreland was one of the goats. The other was Spiro. "I saw my dad after I dropped you off."

"Oh?" I said. I knew he hadn't seen his father for four and a half years.

"I got a letter from him last month," he said. "He asked me to come see him. Said he'd been doing a lot of thinking since he got fired."

"We spent the whole weekend together, and you never told me you'd heard from him?" I said.

"I wasn't sure what I was gonna do," he said. "I didn't make up my mind till after I left you off."

A Philadelphia cop for many years, Ritchie's father had suddenly found himself getting transferred from one district to another, two weeks here, three weeks there, junk jobs and trash details. When he'd asked his supervisor what was going on, the man had told him, "Your son's an embarrassment to the department."

"My kid isn't in the department," he'd said.

"You raised him," the captain had said. This was after Ritchie and some other vets had barricaded themselves inside the Statue of Liberty, unfurling an upside down American flag, the international signal for distress, from Lady Liberty's crown. It had made news all over the world. Ritchie's father had put up with the harassment for awhile longer, then he'd quit. They hadn't actually fired him, but they had shown him the door and made it clear what would happen if he didn't walk through it, so it amounted to the same thing.

"That got to him," Ritchie said. "'Shit like this isn't supposed to happen in America,' he's thinking. Then all this Watergate shit starts coming down, and he started payin' attention. You know what he told me? 'You were right,' he said, 'You were right all along.' So then I asked him why he never told me what combat would be like, and he said, 'Because I always thought it was worth it. I've always been proud I served my country. I thought that was just the price you had to pay. I was proud you were going.' Then he started crying. I never saw my old man cry in all my life. I'm gonna take Kate and the boys up in a few weeks. I want Kate to hear Dad's rap. Maybe she'll understand why I've been so pissed off ever since I got back."

"You two still having trouble?" I said.

"Not since we moved here," he said. "But she's still sore about it. Can you blame her? There she was with a newborn infant and a husband who was getting arrested every other week. House all the time full of stoned vets on their way from one demonstration to the next. I didn't know who half of them were. You can't expect her to understand. She waited a whole year for me, and when I got back, I wasn't me."

After awhile, we went around back and started weeding the garden. Jonathan was swinging on the swing Ritchie had hung from a tree. David crawled around in the garden, pulling up carrots and trying to eat them, though he didn't have enough teeth yet to make much progress. Kate was in the backyard doing laundry in a large tub.

"Paul Mason was here last week," Ritchie said.

114

"I haven't seen him since the trial ended," I said. "How's he doing?"

"Not so hot," he said.

Mason was one of the so-called Gainesville Eight, a group of Vietnam veterans who'd been arrested in August 1972 and charged with conspiring to blow up the 1972 Republican National Convention with firebombs, automatic weapons, and slingshots. Really. Slingshots. That's what the charge sheet had said. It had been front-page news. Fourteen months later, after Nixon and Agnew had been renominated and re-elected on a platform of law and order, the judge had dismissed the charges. He said the government had no case and never should have brought it to trial. That had been worth two paragraphs on page eighteen, buried among the hog futures and wedding announcements.

A former army lieutenant with a Bronze Star and a Cross of Gallantry, Mason had been fired from his job as an auto parts store manager when he'd been arrested, and when he'd tried to get his job back after the trial, the company had told him they were sorry but they couldn't just fire his replacement for no reason. He'd lost all his savings and gone heavily into debt to pay his legal fees, and he hadn't been able to find another job since.

"What's he gonna do?" I said.

"He was headed for Texas," Ritchie said. "He's got a cousin there who thinks maybe he can get him a job as a night watchman."

"A night watchman in Texas," I said.

"And that's only maybe," said Ritchie. "Maybe."

"'Crazed Viet Vets Plan Bloodbath,'" I said. "They got what they wanted. Headlines. They wanted to make the dumb-fuck Silent Majority believe that the whole antiwar movement was a bunch of violence junkies out to destroy America. And it worked, too, didn't it?"

"You know what I'd like to do, don't you?" said Ritchie. "After the revolution, baby."

"Crazed Viet Vets Plan Bloodbath," I said, picking up a zuchini and looking it over as if I were checking for wires.

"That's why I like it here," he said.

"Nice place you got here," I said.

"You want to come and stay for awhile?"

"Kate would love that."

"We could fix up the shed," he said, "Make a little room for you. I've been thinking about getting a few cows, maybe put in some more corn and try a little wheat. I could use the help."

"You serious?"

"Yeh."

"My attorney wants me to go to law school," I said.

"Law school?" he said.

"I gotta do something," I said.

"Why don't you come here?"

"On the other hand, if the Honorable Xavier R. Francis and his pals get their way, I may not be going anywhere for awhile."

*　　*　　*

"You weren't a company plant, were you?" Roger asked. I pulled the receiver away from my ear and looked at it.

"Roger the Engineer wouldn't ask me a thing like that," I said loud enough for him to hear. Then I put it back to my ear.

"Sorry," he said. "It's been driving me nuts. Nobody has any idea who blew the whistle. The whole fleet's been trying to figure it out, but whoever it was is doing a low crawl. He damn well better, too. If we ever find out, over the side on a moonless night off Sitka with an anchor up his ass."

"Doing a low crawl?" I said.

"I learned that from you," he said.

"How've you been?"

"Okay. I've been home for two months, but I just got assigned to the *Pacific Challenger*. I leave next week. Sailing isn't much fun these days. Everybody's tight as a drum. Nobody trusts anybody. Stupid company. It was safer when we were all stoned. I

116

won't be surprised if some young helmsman runs us onto the rocks cold sober just for spite."

"It'll blow over eventually," I said. "I'd rather be there than here."

"We had some times, didn't we?" he said. "Remember the time we threw your mattress overboard?"

"Maybe you can't run away from your problems," I said. "But you can always throw them overboard."

On my first morning on the tanker, when I was a messman in the steward's department, the second cook had told me to throw out the garbage. He was a gruff Filipino with a pot belly who always carried a huge carving knife in one hand and cooked with a cigarette dangling from his lips. I stepped onto the fantail where eleven garbage cans stood brimming from three days in port. I looked around for a place to dump them, but saw nothing.

"What do I do with this stuff?" I had asked.

"Put it in your locker," he had said, his tone of voice suggesting that I was the stupidest person he had yet encountered in a long and sordid life. I dumped the garbage over the side.

Life at sea had been very simple, and most problems had simple solutions. Everything went over the side: leftover ox tail soup and cucumber salad, five-gallon cardboard ice cream cartons and plastic half-gallon orange juice containers, bacon drippings and old magazines and eggshells by the ton. When I switched to the engine department, twice a day I would empty the engineroom trash: metal shavings, oily rags, old batteries, electrical wiring, burned-out lightbulbs, it all went over the side. One morning my clock-radio had broken, so I'd opened the porthole and thrown it over the side. Roger and I had thrown my extra mattress and springs over the side one night in the Straits of Juan de Fuca to make room for a new stereo set. Roger had thrown his dope over the side and he still had his job. About the only thing that didn't get thrown overboard was the oil we carried. That, and my dope.

"I got your letter," said Roger. "I could vouch for you on the night before the raid, but once they get me on the witness stand under oath, what do I tell them when they ask me if I ever smoked with you?"

"You take the Fifth."

"You know what the company will do with that, don't you?"

"They can't lift your license for that."

"Maybe not, but they can fire me," he said. "You think the union's gonna back me up?"

"No," I said. "No."

"I need this job."

"Don't worry about it. I can use the gate log."

"You sure?"

"Yeh," I said. I wasn't, but Roger had a wife and a child. "Be careful out there," I said. "Ramos chirped like a bird."

"How do you know?"

"I read a statement he gave the Coast Guard. He had us dropping acid, shooting heroin, snorting coke, chewing betel nut, and doing the antler dance on the boat deck dressed in pillowcases under a full moon."

"But they only got him for seeds and stems," Roger said. "Why would he do that?"

"Some people aren't smart enough to call a good attorney," I said. "How bright was Ramos? They must have shown him pictures of Attica or beat him with a rubber hose or something, then offered to drop the charges in return for the statement. They probably knew they didn't have much of a case against him, so they figured they could use him to get the rest of us. You know how he explained the seeds and stems? He told 'em I'd come to his cabin the night before and dropped a bag of dope on the floor. He told them I tried to get him to smoke with me, but of course he refused."

"Ramos refused to smoke pot?" said Roger.

"I know," I said.

"You weren't even on the ship the night before the raid," said Roger.

"It doesn't matter. They can't use his statement anyway. It's just hearsay. But he fingered you and just about everybody else on the ship except the search party. And you can bet a copy of his statement went straight to the company before the ink was even dry."

*   *   *

"Thrombophlebitis?" said Daniel. "What kind of a disease is that?"

"It's what you get when you lie," I said. "Pinocchio had it."

"Well, it says here Nixon's got it."

"There you are," I said.

"It also says Rodino's got a smoking gun. The last batch of tapes has Nixon authorizing hush money for Hunt."

"Can you imagine that?"

"They'll have to impeach him now," said Daniel.

"He'll never stand trial," I said. "I bet he resigns first."

"Maybe he'll die of thrombophlebitis."

"I should live to see the day."

"How's your trial coming?"

"Don't ask."

"I already did."

"We don't convene again until August 12th. I'll have to take another day off."

"Don't worry about it," said Daniel. "Are you going to win?"

"Damned if I know. The dickhead judge is bending over backwards to see that I don't. They had a lab report that was so fucked up it didn't even have my name on it. That should have been the ballgame right there. Even my lawyer thought so. But the dickhead prosecutor asks the dickhead judge if he can send the stuff out again to be re-analyzed, and the dickhead judge says yes. That can't possibly be legal, but he did it anyway."

"You can appeal, can't you?"

"I can appeal it all the way to the United States Supreme Court if I want to, but not until the trial is over. Besides, appeals cost money. My money. Your money, too. Have you any idea how much of the taxpayers' money is getting wasted trying to burn me for

119

less dope than one of those marijuana rabbits does up in about three seconds?"

"Look at the bright side," said Daniel. "If they weren't after you, they might be out causing trouble."

"This isn't trouble?" I said.

"You're just stubborn. You should have handed in your ticket and walked away from it."

"And then I could be dealing with the Department of Justice instead of the Department of Transportation. I'd rather get it over with now."

"And what if you lose?"

"Well, yes, there is that."

"Besides, the Feds wouldn't bother with a chickenshit bust like yours."

"Think not?" I said. "Three muckittimucks from the company front office have come all the way from California for each of the first two sessions. They don't do anything but sit there from gavel to gavel impersonating tree stumps. That's a lot of corporate money sitting around on their fat asses. They're obviously very interested in the outcome of this trial. And this is the seventh largest oil company in the world we're talking about. They have clout. You think they would have allowed the Justice Department to ignore me? Here comes a customer. I better get to work before the boss gets mad."

"Hey, I'm the boss," said Daniel. "Get to work. You want me to leave the newspaper?"

"Yes."

"Wanna have dinner with us tonight?"

"Sure. Call Sarah this time, okay?"

While we were eating a few hours later, Sam dropped by to pick up a casserole dish Sarah had borrowed from Jan.

"You don't look so good," said Daniel.

"The Zimmerman jury brought in a verdict this afternoon," said Sam. He was referring to the trial that had been developed with the help of the young cop who had agreed to cooperate with the crime commission and the special prosecutor's office. "Not guilty on all counts."

"I told you so," said Daniel.

"If you were on the jury, and your name and address were a matter of public record, would you vote to send three Philadelphia cops to prison?" I said.

"Pound sand," said Daniel. "What a sucker that guy was. You ruined his life for nothing. He should have taken the money in the first place and told you guys to piss up a rope."

"What are you going to do now?" I said.

"Go home and eat dinner," said Sam.

*   *   *

On August 9th, 1974, Richard Milhous Nixon became the first person ever to resign the presidency of the United States. Days prior to Nixon's resignation, the Rodino Committee had finally voted out three articles of impeachment for obstruction of justice, abuse of the powers of the presidency, and unconstitutional refusal of congressional subpoenas. Two additional articles for the secret bombing of Cambodia and Nixon's personal financial practices—among them an Arnold Palmer putting green at his Key Biscayne residence paid for with laundered campaign funds—had failed to carry. Before the full House of Representatives could vote on the three articles that had carried in committee, Nixon had taken his $60,000 pension, $96,000 for office expenses and staff, $18,000 civil service retirement benefits, Secret Service protection, free office space, free mail, free government transportation, and exercised the greater part of valor.

During the same week, former senator Wayne Morse, one of only two members of Congress to vote against Lyndon Johnson's Gulf of Tonkin Resolution back in 1964, died at age seventy-three, having been voted out of office in 1968, the year Nixon was first elected president; a senate report charged South Vietnamese army officers with selling $36 million worth of used U.S. artillery shell casings for scrap metal on the black market and pocketing the proceeds; and Spiro Agnew, Nixon's vice president until he'd pleaded no contest to charges of extortion and income tax evasion the previous year, was granted a permit to carry a handgun in spite of his felony conviction because, the court ruled, he was "not likely to act in a manner dangerous to public safety."

"Are you happy now?" said Richards on the way to our next hearing session.

"Am I missing something?" I said.

"Nixon," he said.

"They should have impeached him anyway," I said.

"Are you ever satisfied?"

"Is it too much to ask that he spend a day or two in jail? Just one photograph of him in a striped suit for the sake of posterity? He was supposed to be finished in 1952. He was supposed to be washed up in 1962. Somewhere down the pike, he'll be resurrected as a great statesman dragged down by the nattering nabobs of negativism."

"I wouldn't be too sure about that," said Richards. "He's still an unindicted co-conspirator. I think Jaworski'll file criminal charges against him." Leon Jaworski was the Watergate special prosecutor.

"Never happen," I said. "He cut a deal with Ford when he made him vice president. Ford won't let that happen. He'll pardon him first if he has to."

"He can't do that," said Richards. "It would be political suicide."

"What does Ford care?" I said. "He was just a Congressman with a secure seat. Maybe he could have been Speaker of the House some day, but that's as high as he was ever going to get. And now he's president of the United States. You think he cares if he gets re-elected? He's set for life. You wait and see. Did you find out what this judge is up to?"

"The second lab report might be admissible if Blavitt can prove an airtight chain of custody," said Richards. "I don't think he can do that, but we'll find out today."

An hour later we were underway. Again the three company executives were the only spectators in the courtroom. Blavitt opened by introducing the lab report from the Philadelphia police lab.

"Objection, your honor," said Richards. "The chain of custody has not yet been established."

"Why don't you introduce the chain of custody, Mister Blavitt?" said the judge.

"He's not allowed to coach Blavitt like that, is he?" I said.

"Be quiet," said Richards.

"I was just about to do that, your honor," said Blavitt, and he did.

"Objection, your honor," said Richards. "This purported chain of custody is deficient both on its face and due to its incompleteness."

"Would you care to elaborate, counsellor?" said the judge.

"I would appreciate the opportunity, your honor. The opening entry is dated April 5th, 1974, but the alleged evidence was seized on March 6th. There's no documentation for the intervening time."

"Special Agent Leaderman has already testified to that," said Blavitt.

"He said the alleged evidence was kept in a safe to which three other people besides himself had access," said Richards. "Unless we have the opportunity to question each of these three people, we have no way of knowing what each of these people did or did not do with respect to the alleged evidence in this case. Our inability to cross-examine is a denial of due process, your honor. In addition, the endorsement transferring the alleged evidence from Special Agent Leaderman to Lieutenant Purcell is not signed by either man. There are only typewritten names. Anyone could have typed those names. This is a clear breach of the chain."

"Mister Leaderman already testified that he personally delivered the evidence to Lieutenant Purcell," said Blavitt.

"Alleged evidence, your honor," said Richards. "Mister Leaderman testified that he delivered the alleged evidence to the Coast Guard. To whom did he deliver it? He made no mention of

Lieutenant Purcell or any other individual. Moreover, this document states that Lieutenant Purcell delivered the alleged evidence to a James Quinn at the UCLA medical lab on April 8th and received it back on April 19th, but there is no signature for Mister Quinn, only a typed name in each instance. Again, this is a clear breach in the chain of custody. Again, where is our opportunity to cross-examine? The next endorsement is the signature of Lieutenant Commander Jarvis. Who is he and what is he doing with the alleged evidence? There is no indication, and there has been no testimony from or about him."

"He's the senior investigating officer in Long Beach, your honor," said Blavitt.

"But where is the documentation? Where is our opportunity to cross-examine? The next entry indicates that the alleged evidence was sent on April 30th to Philadelphia marked "Senior Investigating Officer Only," but the registered letter purporting to effect that transfer carries no such notation. Who actually received and opened the material? There is no indication. Another break in the chain."

"Commander Jeffries received the letter and its contents," said Blavitt.

"Where is his signature?" asked Richards. "I don't see it here."

"That can easily be remedied, your honor," said Blavitt.

"How did the alleged evidence get from Commander Jeffries to this courtroom, your honor?"

"He personally gave it to me," said Blavitt, "I brought it here."

"For all three sessions?"

"Yes."

"Where is his endorsement? Or yours? Where has the material been kept since it arrived in Philadelphia? There's no indication of that."

"I kept it in our safe," said Blavitt.

"How many other people have access to that safe?" asked Richards.

"Five or six others," said Blavitt.

"Who are they?" asked Richards. "We've had no opportunity to examine them. Finally, who has been responsible for the alleged evidence during breaks and recesses in this proceeding? At least three strangers have had access to this courtroom during previous sessions, and they are present again today."

"I think we can safely assume that the evidence has not been tampered with during the actual hearings," said the judge.

"With all due respect, your honor," said Richards, "I don't think the law allows us to assume anything."

"I'll take responsibility for that," said the judge.

"Be that as it may, your honor, my objection stands. There are numerous breaks in the supposed chain of custody that can be remedied only by the testimony of witnesses which the prosecution has not called to the stand. Due process requires no less. The rules of evidence on chain of custody are quite clear, and this document does not meet those rules."

"I will allow the letter to be entered for identification only," the judge said, "though I reserve the right to rule on its validity at a later date."

"Your honor," said Blavitt, "I would like to reintroduce the lab report from the Philadelphia police."

"Objection, your honor," said Richards.

"What is your objection, counsellor?" said the judge. He sounded tired.

"I have several, your honor. There's nothing in the chain of custody letter to indicate the transfer of the alleged evidence to and from the Philadelphia Police Department. In addition, the items specified in the charge sheet differ markedly from this new lab report. The lab report makes no mention of a Sucrets container, a baggie, a cigar tube, or seven marijuana cigarettes, and it gives the total weight of the material as only five and a half grams, not the eleven grams my client is charged with."

"There was no need to analyze the containers, and the quantity is not at issue here," said Blavitt. "The material itself is the issue. Handling and testing could account for the discrepancy."

"Perhaps the police chemist could speak to that, your honor," said Richards. "I was under the impression he would be available for testimony today."

"Mister Blavitt?" said the judge.

"I didn't think it would be necesary," said Blavitt.

"You didn't think it would be necessary," said the judge.

"Your honor, I submit this new lab report is inadmissible," said Richards.

"I'll be the judge of that," said the judge. "I'll accept it for identification only at this time. Does the government have anything further?"

"No, your honor," said Blavitt, "The government rests its case."

"Counsellor, are you ready to present your defense?"

"Your honor, I move that the case against my client be dismissed for the following reasons: the chain of custody has not been established, the initial lab report has no bearing on my client whatsoever, and the second lab report is invalid because of prior breaks in the chain of custody. Moreover, this whole action has been taken pursuant to 46 USC 239 a and b, but section 239 b (b) (2) specifies that revocation of a merchant mariner's document can be effected only if the seaman is a user of or addicted to the use of a narcotic drug. My client is not charged with use or addiction, but with possession, about which the statute is silent. I question whether possession has been established, since neither witness testified that the alleged contraband was found on the physical person of my client. But in any case, all of the testimony pertains to possession alone. The presence of drugs in an individual's room does not in itself constitute use or addiction. Finally, there are in fact five different types of marijuana, only one of which, *L Cannibis*, has been defined by federal statute as an illegal narcotic. Not one document, including two different lab reports, makes any mention of *L Cannibis*. Incorporating all of the above, your honor, I respectfully move that this case be dismissed on the grounds that the prosecution has failed to establish a *prima facie* case against my client."

"I would like to take a brief recess in order to consider your motion," said the judge. "We'll reconvene in fifteen minutes." Then he stood up and walked out.

"I sounded pretty convincing, didn't I?" said Richards.

"You sounded pretty convincing the last time, too," I said.

"Oh ye of little faith. He's got to rule in your favor. He's already admitted that the initial lab report is deficient. He can't bring himself to admit that the chain of custody is flawed, but he knows it is. And the second lab report is worthless without a valid chain of custody. Did you see the look he gave Blavitt when Blavitt told him the police chemist wasn't here?"

"I like the way he takes responsibility for the integrity of the evidence in his courtroom," I said, pointing to the pile of evidence sitting in front of the judge's table, "then gets up and walks out."

"Here comes the judge," said Richards. Actually, what he said was, "Here come de judge."

"If you'll bear with me, gentlemen," the judge said, "I need more time to consider this motion than present circumstances allow. We'll reconvene on September 9th. Counsellor, be prepared to present your defense at that time, should it be necessary." Then he banged his little gavel, stood up, and walked out.

"September 9th?" I said. "That's another four weeks. He can't do that."

"Yes, he can," said Richards, "but it's all over. He knows he's got no choice, but he's having a hard time of it because there's no doubt in his mind that you're guilty. He's angry that the Coast Guard has botched this so badly. He needs time to steel himself to do what he knows he has to do."

"If you ask me, he just wants to leave me twisting slowly, slowly in the wind for as long as possible," I said.

"No doubt there's a little of that, too," said Richards. "But that's okay because you'll have the last laugh."

"You're sure of that," I said.

"Pretty sure."

"What do you mean, pretty sure?"

"Anything can happen in a courtroom," said Richards.

*   *   *

The MG was a lot zippier than my Volkswagen had been, but it was far less dependable. The VW had traveled 122,000 miles without ever leaving me stranded in America. The MG broke down when it felt like it.

I was driving to Cape Cod on Labor Day weekend to see Roger the Engineer. He'd decided to take another month of vacation and go out on the *Pride of Chester*. On the Garden State Parkway, I kept smelling a foul odor. I figured it was the fumes of North Jersey, as fine an indictment of the Industrial Revolution as ever there was, but when I slowed down for a toll plaza, steam boiled up from under the engine cover and the floorboard. It stank like hell.

I cut the engine and coasted over to the shoulder. A hose had split. I left the engine cover up and rooted through the boot to see if I had any duct tape. I didn't. I sat down on the rear bumper. Four lanes of cars streamed steadily by. It was almost dark. Nobody stopped. Finally a cop car turned on its revolving light as it approached, then pulled up behind me. I stood up, but even before I was fully erect, a New Jersey state trooper leaped out of the car with his gun drawn and pointed at me. Oh fuck, I thought. My hands went straight up before he had finished saying, "Get your hands up! Don't move!"

"My car broke," I said.

"Put your hands on the back of the car," he barked. I assumed the position. He patted me down. "Put your hands behind your back. Slowly." He snapped a pair of handcuffs on me. Then he ordered me over to his car and stuffed me in the back seat. He kept his gun on me while he reached in, grabbed his radio handset, and called for a back-up. He referred to me as "the suspect."

"Do you mind telling me what I'm suspected of?" I asked when he'd replaced the handset. He didn't get into the car, but stood pointing his gun at me through the open back door.

"Yeh, I mind," he said.

"I'm not who you think I am," I said. "I can prove who I am, and I'm not whoever you're looking for."

"You'll get your chance," he said. Another cop car pulled up behind us. The cop who'd busted me got behind the wheel and one of the other cops got in the front on the passenger's side, then we pulled out with the other car following us.

"What about my car?" I said.

"It won't go anywhere," the driver said. They took me about ten miles to a state police barracks, cuffed me to a chair, and started down the list. They emptied my wallet.

"You speak Spanish?" asked the cop who seemed to be in charge. He was a powerfully built man with blonde wavy hair and a jutting jaw. He looked like Dudley Dooright of the Royal Canadian Mounted Police.

"Not really," I said. "I had two years in high school, but I only got a C on the final exam."

"You don't speak Spanish?"

"No."

"You sure you weren't in Jersey City last night?"

"Very sure. I worked until nine, then I went home. You can call my boss. I've got his home phone number."

"Where were you around midnight?" asked Dudley.

"In bed," I said. "Asleep."

"I suppose you can prove that," he said. I couldn't. The people who owned the house where I was staying had left the day before for Avalon.

"No, but I'm not who you think I am. Check my fingerprints. My fingerprints are on my merchant seaman's card and my military ID."

"Where did you get a military ID?" he said. There were three other uniformed troopers in the room, and one man in a light blue suit. They were all standing. I had to keep looking up.

"Where do you think I got it? I got it in the Marines."

"You don't look like a Marine," said Dudley.

"I'm an ex-Marine."

"This doesn't look like you," he said, indicating the photo on the card.

"That was taken eight years ago," I said.

"What are you doing with it?"

"I like the picture," I said. "It's flattering, don't you think?" It had been taken about four a.m., a few hours after I'd arrived at Parris Island. The photograph looked like a police mug shot. My eyes stared straight into the camera. My head had been shaved bald. The drill instructors had worn Smokey the Bear hats just like these men wore.

"Your hair's too short," said Dudley, indicating the photo again. "Now it's too long." It wasn't a question, so I didn't say anything. "Do any demolition work in the Marines?" he asked.

"I used C-4 to heat my coffee water, that was about it."

"You heated coffee with plastic explosive?"

"Sure. It won't blow up if it's not under pressure. You need a blasting cap to set it off."

"How do you know that?" said Dudley. He said it as if he had just tripped me up.

"It's just something you pick up," I said. "You see other guys doing it. Lots of times, we couldn't get heat tabs."

"But you know how to detonate it."

"Yes, but I'm not a demolitions expert. I did it maybe once or twice. With a lot of supervision."

"Who was your supervisor, Che Guevara?"

"Who do you think I am? Check my fingerprints. It can't be that hard." I wanted to say, "You look like a bright lad," but I didn't.

Another trooper opened the door, motioned Dudley over, and they had a little conference. The other three men stared at me, as if they expected me to turn into the Incredible Hulk. Then Dudley came back and took off the handcuffs.

"Okay, your story checks out," he said.

"It's not a story," I said. "Who did you think I was?"

"That's no business of yours," he said.

"Gimme a break," I said. "You drag me off at gunpoint and chain me to a chair, keep me here for three hours, and it's not my business?"

"We're looking for a Puerto Rican terrorist," he said.

"Do I look Puerto Rican? Do I sound Puerto Rican? What on earth made you think I was a Puerto Rican terrorist?"

"We had a report that he'd been seen on the Parkway."

"It's a big road," I said.

"Trooper Hanson will take you back to your car," said Dudley. He was the cop who'd busted me. As we pulled back onto the parkway, I asked him the same questions I'd asked Dudley.

"We have to take precautions," said Trooper Hanson. He didn't take his eyes off the road in front of him.

"Listen to my voice. Do I sound Puerto Rican?"

"You want me to take you back to the barracks and you can discuss it with Lieutenant Cobb?" he said.

"Francis Marion was a terrorist," I said. "Ask any English school-boy."

We rode the rest of the way in silence. When we got back to my car, all four tires were gone. The trunk had been pried open, and the spare was gone, too. I found a telephone and called Jim Best. Then I called Roger and told him I wasn't coming.

"The New Jersey state police stole your tires?" said Roger.

"Might as well have," I said.

By the time Jim and I got the MG off the parkway, it was too late to get any tires, so I stayed at his place that night. He lived in Montclair with his wife and infant son. After he resigned from West Point and served out the remainder of his enlistment, he'd gone to work as a researcher for a New York City television station, but when he began to get his name in the newspapers as a spokesperson for Vietnam Veterans Against the War, they fired him. They didn't tell him that. They told him they were phasing

131

out his position. But they'd hired somebody else the next day, and he hadn't been able to find work as a journalist anywhere in the city. After six years, he'd left Brooklyn and found a job as a stringer for a Bergen County daily.

"You're lucky I didn't have an assignment tonight," he said.

"You're not," I said. He only got paid when he worked. "How's the job?"

"I get to listen to a lot of people argue," he said. "Town councils, zoning hearing boards, water and sewer authorities. They send me someplace different every night. I never know what's going on. It's like a VVAW meeting."

"What happened to the revolution, Jim? We were right there. We were right on the edge. There were four hundred thousand people at Woodstock. Not a single gun in the crowd. Not one life lost. Not even a fistfight. Five loaves and two fishes, and nobody went away hungry. How could they stop us?"

"We made a mistake," he said. "We thought they would listen, but people with power don't have to listen. Send you to Vietnam. Send you to prison. Makes no difference to them. They didn't get where they are by playing badminton. But they made a mistake, too. They didn't kill us all. Look at these." He pulled out a fat folder of papers. "People have been sending these from all over the country. Look at this letter. 'I served with the 307th Aviation Battalion in Vietnam, and I just read your book of poems. It felt like I'd found a brother. Keep the faith.' Look at this one; it's a poem. 'You have taught me to love those whom I fought and was once taught to hate, and to question that love which I used to blindly obey, and to serve no one or no thing blindly ever again.' Hundreds of them. Vets. Draft resisters. Parents. School kids. We touched people. That book touched people. Want to help me do another one?"

"Don't you ever get tired?" I said.

"Can you forget everything you learned in Vietnam?" he said. "Can you forget everything you've learned since? Do you have any choice?"

"That's why I went to sea," I said.

"Well, you're not at sea anymore, are you? What will you do when they come for your kid? 'Here's a gun, kid. Go kill those people over there.'"

"I don't have a kid."

"What about my kid? What about Ritchie's kids? You know what you know. The only choice you have is what you're going to do with it."

*   *   *

"I lost five tires this time," I said. "I had to hire a special truck to get my car off the parkway. And my trunk's wrecked. Puerto Rican terrorist, for chrissake. Fucking pigs."

"Fucking pigs," said Richards. "Now that's diplomacy."

"I'm not a diplomat," I said.

"You can say that again."

"Robert, I did not do anything wrong. My car broke down. I was just sitting there waiting for help. You don't believe me, do you?"

"I know you have a bad habit of asking for trouble," he said.

"No, I don't ask for it. You're not willing to see it, but there's a war going on out there, Robert. Vietnam stripped the clothes right off the emperor's back, and they're desperate to get him dressed up again, damn the constitution, damn the bill of rights, damn the torpedoes."

"You don't believe me either," he said. "I've told you before, I see more than you think I do, but I don't think it's as bad as you think it is."

"Have you ever had someone point a loaded weapon at you? It makes your heart beat really fast. It sucks the air right out of your lungs. It makes you angry. Sooner or later, I'm going to meet an eager cop or the end of my patience, and then I'm going to be dead. And for what? For looking scruffy?"

"You can do something about it," Richards said.

133

"Yes. Move to England. The cops don't carry guns in England."

"They do now, I think."

"It figures."

"Have you signed up for the law boards yet?"

"That's your solution?" I said.

"It's a start," he said. "You want things to change overnight. What you have to do is roll up your sleeves and dig in your heels. People get caught in the gears all the time, as you say, but you can help them."

"Smash the fucking machinery. That would help."

"That's not likely to happen soon."

"I know."

"Then why don't you concentrate on something that is likely to happen? Where do you think your Miranda rights came from? Some lawyer took the police to court and won. You can do that, too, but you've got to start somewhere. All you have to do is take the law boards, don't fall asleep while you're taking them, and you've got your start."

"I'm supposed to take them later this month."

"Good."

"You think so? Did you see what happened in the Zimmerman trial?"

"Yes," he said.

"They all walked."

"Sometimes the system works, but you only notice when it doesn't. Look how many of the Watergate conspirators have gone to prison. Erlichman just got twenty months to five years."

"In Allenwood," I said. "Or did he get Lompoc? He'll do six months, maybe eight, max. And he'll sit on the sundeck and while away the hours between conjugal visits writing the book he's already gotten a six-figure advance for. Or was that Haldeman? It doesn't matter. Erlichman will get a book contract, too. Hunt's got one. Colson's got one. Donald Segretti has a book contract, for crying out loud. They're all getting rich off Watergate."

"These were powerful men," said Richards. "They've been humiliated and stripped of their power. You can't begin to calculate the severity of a sentence like that."

"Spiro Agnew does look like a chastened man playing golf in Palm Springs with Frank Sinatra, don't you think?"

"We've got to get going or we'll miss our train," he said. He began grabbing folders and legal pads off his desk and stuffing them into his briefcase.

"What are we going to do if the judge denies our motion?" I said.

"I don't see how he can."

"But what if he does?"

"We'll go through the interrogatories and work on the fact that your cabin was accessible to several dozen people during most of the time the ship was in Long Beach."

"That's not much of a defense," I said.

"We only have to establish reasonable doubt," he said. "Anyway, I don't think it'll come to that."

"I thought you always worried until the verdict is in."

"I do."

"On the pending motion to dismiss," said the judge an hour and a half later, "Both the master of the vessel and the special agent for the shipping company testified as to their search of the defendant's room and what they found there. They could not state what the suspected substances were, only what they suspected them to be. Such opinion are not evidence. Therefore the suspected substances were submitted to a chemical laboratory for analysis via a chain of custody.

"The evidence offered to establish the chain of custody was exhibit seven. Each of those through whose hands the alleged evidence passed are named, but the so-called chain of custody is a mixture of signed and typewritten names. Nobody's testimony in the chain was taken, and the alleged chain, namely exhibit seven itself, is not *prima facie* evidence of continuous custody.

"The lab report from the UCLA medical lab speaks of marijuana being in four envelopes without identifying any envelope as

135

belonging to any particular crew member. The report itself does not mention the name of the defendant.

"Exhibit seven speaks of the envelopes being delivered to the UCLA medical lab with seals intact, and then being redelivered to the Coast Guard with seals intact. Does this mean that the seals were never opened and the contents of the envelopes never analyzed?

"Exhibit seven speaks of envelopes being delivered to the UCLA medical lab by the Coast Guard. Exhibit eight, the lab report itself, says the samples were submitted by the U.S. Marines. Exhibit eight does not speak of marijuana cigarettes; neither does it mention a Sucrets container. It gives the weight of the marijuana as twenty-two grams. The second specification of the charge speaks of ten grams, and the third speaks of one. Exhibit eleven, the lab report from the Philadelphia police lab, refers to 4.5 grams, residue of marijuana, and also .5 grams and seven paper packets in the form of cigarettes.

"Viewed in the proper technical light, there is grave doubt about the veracity of the evidence by reason of the breaks in the chain of custody and apparent errors in the laboratory report. This doubt must be resolved in favor of the defendant. The attempt by the investigating officer to overcome the infirmities of the original lab report by a second analysis is unsuccessful because of the breaks in the chain of custody.

"Therefore, it is the order of this court that the charges and specifications herein are dismissed. This hearing is adjourned," said the judge. Then he banged his little gavel.

"Sometimes it works," said Richards.

I stood up and turned around. The director of marine personnel, who had hired me more than a year earlier and who had sat through all four sessions like a vulture waiting to pick the corpse, was glaring at me, his eyes riveted as if to something fascinating and repugnant. Silently but clearly, I mouthed the words, "Fuck you." When I turned back, Blavitt was standing next to me.

"Well," he said, "I hope you've learned something from all of this."

136

"I bet you learned a lot more than I did," I said. "Let's get out of here, Robert." Richards and I went to the coffeeshop across the street. "But it didn't work," I said. "I was guilty as charged, and you knew it all along. How could you keep a straight face?"

"You did," he said.

"I didn't have to say anything."

"Don't you think justice was served?" he asked.

"I think justice was served, but nobody else in that room does."

"I do," he said. "You're probably right about marijuana. You're the expert, but I haven't seen anything yet to make me think you're wrong. I've never said our laws are just. But I do believe a society without laws is worse than one with unjust laws. And the best way to check the power of the state is the exercise we've just been through. The state charged you with breaking the law, but they broke the law too. And when the state breaks the law, it scares me far more than when you do. Today the state got a lesson that it, too, is subject to the rule of law. I'd say justice was served very nicely."

"They took my job," I said. "And they still owe me two weeks' pay and two months' paid vacation."

"That's the lesson you got," he said. "You think the marijuana laws are stupid, so you ignored them. Richard Nixon ignored the law, too. Sooner or later, everyone pays a price. I believe that."

"You can't possibly equate what I did with what Nixon did," I said.

"Of course not," he said, "except in the sense that no individual has the right to choose which laws he'll obey and which ones he'll disregard. Society can't function like that. I don't mean it shouldn't. I mean it can't. If you think a particular law is unjust, you work to change it. The beauty of our system is that it allows for that kind of change."

"And what do you do when you can't even get a hearing?" I said.

"What are you thinking of?"

"A few years ago, a guy named John David Herndon deserted

from the army because he had orders for Vietnam. He argued that the orders were invalid because the war itself was illegal. Rather than court-martial him and risk testing his argument, the army simply discharged him."

"That's a different problem," he said. "The law itself wasn't in question."

"But what do you do about that? What do you do when the state breaks the rules and the entire institutional mechanism of the state refuses to address it, let alone redress it?"

"You do exactly what you did," he said. "You take to the streets. You hound your representatives. You get as many people as you can to push as hard as they can in any way they can think of until something gives. And something did give. How many American soldiers were in Vietnam when you were there?"

"Close to half a million, but—"

"And how many are there now?"

"More than there ought to be, only now they're called civilian contractors and nobody cares."

"But what if there had been no limits on the state?" he said. "What would Nixon, or Johnson before him, have done to that country?"

"Maybe the war would have ended long before it's going to," I said. "At least when American kids were coming home in garbage bags, people paid attention. Now it's only Asians dying."

"It isn't a perfect world," he said. "Maybe the war would have ended sooner. Maybe not. You see the way things are and imagine better. I see the way things are and imagine worse. Maybe the world needs both of us."

"You did a good job for me, Robert. Thanks."

"It's been fun, hasn't it?"

"Fun?"

"I've had a ball. Watching that judge render his decision just now was worth the price of admission. My God, how he hated to have to do that. Maybe we didn't change the world today, but we sure stuck it to 'em, didn't we? They'll dream about you."

I took out my merchant seaman's card and turned it over in my hands. "Not that it matters," I said.

"You said yourself that wasn't the point," said Richards.

*　　　*　　　*

That same day Gerald Ford, the first president never to be elected president, pardoned Richard Nixon for any and all crimes he may have committed while occupying the White House. Nixon would never sit in the dock. He would never be convicted of high crimes and misdemeanors, or even of jaywalking. He would keep his buttons and epaulets. At least I had faced my accusers. I had never lied about what I had done or why.

So what, I thought. What makes you think that anyone should care? Nixon'll be in the history books, not you. Whatever you think the world owes you, you won't get it. What are you going to do?

"Where's Ray?" I asked Daniel when I got to work the next day.

"He joined the Marines," said Daniel.

"He didn't give any notice?"

"Nope. He came by yesterday afternoon and said he'd just signed the papers. Nice kid, but dumb."

"No dumber than I was."

"That's not saying much," said Daniel.

"No, I guess it isn't," I said.

"Can you work some extra hours until I can hire somebody?"

"Sure," I said.

"We're going canoeing in the Pine Barrens with Sam and Jan on Saturday," he said. "Wanna come?"

"Sure," I said.

We rented canoes at Atsion. The river ran swiftly into the trackless cedar groves, looping back on itself over and over again, cutting into the sandy soil. We had to stop sometimes to free ourselves from sunken stumps or trees that had toppled into the water where the current had eroded the banks. When we drifted, there was no sound but wind in the trees, a sparkle of birdsong, and the gurgling water.

I had always loved water. I had spent my childhood chasing snakes and frogs and painted turtles through the lily pads in Branch Creek. I had been one of the first kids in town to learn the butterfly stroke, and had won a gold medal at the league championships when I was twelve. I had often gone to the Jersey shore, and had become a proficient bodysurfer.

Once, a patrol I was on had emerged from the wasteland of mines and boobytraps we called the Dunes to stand at the edge of the South China Sea. I had waded in to my hips, the easy swells trying to lift me up and set me free, knowing that if only I were strong enough, I could lay down my rifle, peel off my filthy clothes, and swim steadily east until I reached home.

I could not know that when I got there something would be changed, that home would be as distant as that beach at Phuoc Trac, where men and women mended nets and caulked their boats and looked at me as if I wasn't there. Where home should have been, I discovered the same bewildering faces, the same cold, the lay of the land hostile and strange.

At a small beach left by the river as it cut away the opposite bank, we stopped for lunch.

"Weren't you supposed to take your law boards today?" Sam asked, handing me a ham sandwich.

"This sounded like more fun," I said.

"My boss told me I can hire an assistant," he said. "You want the job?"

"What's the job?" I said.

"Custodian of evidence."

"Well, I've certainly learned a few things about the rules of evidence in the past six months."

"That's why I asked," he said.

"I'll think about it," I said.

*   *   *

"Well, actually, Mom, I didn't take the law boards," I said.

"Oh," said my mother. She looked crestfallen. "Why not?"

"The Kaufmans invited me to go canoeing in the Pine Barrens," I said. "That sounded like more fun than sitting indoors taking a test for six hours."

"You couldn't have gone canoeing some other time?" she said.

"Mom, I can't see busting my butt for three years in law school just so I can put on a coat and tie every day and get paid. I don't like neckties. They irritate my neck."

"That's not much of a reason," she said.

"Lawyers are officers of the court, Mom. They have to swear an oath of fealty. The last time I did that, I ended up in Vietnam."

"That's different," she said.

"Is it? How can I swear an oath to uphold and defend a system I have not one ounce of respect for?"

"You were happy enough when the system worked to your benefit," she said.

"No, I wasn't happy about it. They made up the game. They made up the rules. They said, 'Play or else.' They could have sent me to prison, Mom. To prison. For smoking pot. You know what it says on the back of my Purple Heart Medal? 'For Military Merit.' I'm guilty, all right. I'm guilty of murder, attempted murder, arson, assault and battery, aggravated assault, assault with a deadly weapon, robbery, burglary, larceny, disorderly conduct, you name it, I've done it. And according to our so-called system, it was all perfectly legal. They gave me a medal for it. Am I relieved about the way the trial turned out? Yes. Am I happy about it? Not hardly."

My mother started to say something, then stopped.

"All those people ever wanted was for me and my friends to stop killing them and go away. Most of them didn't know one 'ism' from the next. They just wanted to plant their rice and raise their kids and live long enough to bounce their grandchildren on their

141

knees. Just like you, Mom. No different than you. What we've done to them is a crime. And who's standing trial for that? If there's a God in heaven, She'll never forgive us. Not me. Not you. Not any of us."

"You weren't talking like this when you came home," she said.

"I wasn't talking at all," I said. "But you knew something was wrong, didn't you? You knew it from the moment I walked in that door. I can remember you sitting right over there in the easy chair a couple of days later. 'What's wrong?' you asked. 'What is it?' Remember that? Remember?"

"I remember," she said quietly.

"I didn't know how to say it then. I didn't know that Ho Chi Minh went to Versaille in 1919 to ask Woodrow Wilson to help him get the French out of his country, but Wilson wouldn't even give him the time of day. I didn't know the Viet Minh were our allies in World War Two. I didn't know the Republic of Vietnam didn't exist until the United States government invented it. I didn't know that American soldiers burned villages and shot children in the Philippines seventy years ago. I didn't know that the CIA over-threw the only democractically elected government Guatemala ever had because that government wanted United Fruit Company to stop stealing their wealth, or that the secretary of state was on the board of directors of United Fruit Company, or that the di-rector of the CIA was a partner in the law firm that represented United Fruit Company. They didn't teach me stuff like that at Pennridge High School. Do you want me to go on? There's more. Lots more."

There were tears welling up in my mother's eyes. She didn't even try to answer me. A kind and decent person who had never wished anyone harm, she had been a part of the beast for so long that she couldn't begin to tell where she stopped and the beast began. I put my arms around her. The tears rolled down her cheeks like silent sorrows only a mother would understand. She could not imagine that her son was a murderer, this tiny helpless child she had brought forth out of her own body. She could not imagine that she had delivered him into the hands of men so arrogant and ruthless and cynical they would rather lay waste to millions of lives than concede that the world was not theirs to do with as they pleased. But she knew that her son was not stupid. She could neither dismiss me nor reconcile me with what she wanted to believe. I cried, too. I wanted my father to share this moment with us, but I knew that he was too hobbled by his own ghosts to try to understand mine.

"It's okay, Mom," I said. "They didn't teach you any of that stuff either."

"Mister Richards is going to be disappointed," she said.

"He'll get over it. He's a very pragmatic man."

"What are you going to do?"

"I'm not sure, but law school's not the answer. Not for me."

"You know you really can't drive a forklift for the rest of your life."

"Ritchie Lazzarri wants me to move to West Virginia and help him put in some wheat and some more corn. Jim Best wants me to help him edit another poetry anthology. Sam Kaufman asked me to be his assistant at the special prosecutor's office. Right now, I think I'll drive up to the ridge. It's pretty up there at night. Should I take a door key?"

"I'll leave the back door unlocked," she said.

I took the long way up to the cemetery, driving east on Sixth Street, turning right on Callowhill Street, then left onto Branch Road and out of town, left again onto Blooming Glen Road and over one of the last covered bridges in Bucks County, then across Fifth Street out near the high school, then left again on Ridge Road heading back toward town. Like my mother, the people of Perkasie had not intended to do to me or anyone else what they had done. Most of them had not a clue that they had done anything wrong at all. They believed what they believed, and there was little enough in the world they knew to contradict them. Children were born and grew up and got married and had children. Once in awhile, some few of those children died in a war, but the wars were always just and far away, and the dead were not forgotten. That was what Memorial Day was for.

"If you don't like it here," the owner of the Five and Ten had told me one day before I stopped doing business in Perkasie, "why don't you go to Russia?" He was also the mayor. Those who did not believe that Richard Nixon had been hounded from office by a pack of dogs who did not love their country believed that his resignation was living proof that democracy in these United States was alive and healthy.

I parked the car and walked over to Max's grave. Frenchie, Ski, and Bobby were already there.

"I thought I'd find you guys here," I said.

"You won," said Ski. "You beat the rap."

"Yeh, I won," I said.

"You don't sound very happy," he said.

"I'm happier than I would have been if I'd lost."

"What are you gonna do now?" said Frenchie.

"Why does everybody keep asking me that? Tell me something. How come you guys waited so long to show up?"

"Oh, we've been here all along," said Bobby. "You couldn't see us, that's all. You weren't ready. You had to get thrown off that tanker before you started listening. As long as you thought you had a way out, you weren't going to listen to anybody."

"Now ya gotta deal," said Frenchie. "Now you'll listen up."

"You got something to say?" I said.

"Yeh, we got something to say."

"So? Like what?" I said. The three of them looked at each other as if they were the bearers of bad tidings and weren't sure who was going to get stuck with the job of delivering the goods. "Come on. What is it?"

"You know what's going to happen next, don't you?" said Bobby.

"What? You got an exploding cigar? A naked lady in a cake? Stop beating around the bush."

"You know they're gonna come along and say the way the whole

144

thing turned out wasn't their fault," said Ski. "They're gonna say the generals weren't allowed to fight. They're gonna say the bleeding heart press turned the people against the war. They're gonna say the demonstrators destroyed the morale of the troops. They're gonna thump their chests and swing their dicks and stand over our graves waving the fucking flag and say it was all somebody else's fault. They're gonna say we coulda won if only this and only that and blah blah blah. You watch."

"But that's bullshit," I said.

"So what?" he said. "When were you born? What do you think they'll say? 'Sorry, folks, we screwed up and all your kids are dead because of it.'"

"Fat chance," said Frenchie.

"They're gonna turn the whole thing upside down and inside out and every which way but Sunday, and before you can say 'It don't mean nothin',' they're gonna have all those folks down there cryin' in their beers and shoveling their kids off to some other goddamned war in some other godforsaken backwater that never did the good people of Perkasie a lick of harm. You know it's true. What are you going to do about it?"

"What do you expect me to do about it?"

"Say what they won't say," said Bobby. "Say what is."

"I tried that," I said.

"Oh, you tried that," he said. "You make a little noise and when it doesn't work, you shrug your shoulders and walk away."

"You make it sound like nothing. I spent five years trying. I'm tired. I just want to live."

"So did we," said Ski.

"That's below the belt, Ski. I've got enough grief already without you guys piling on. I thought you were my pals."

"We are your pals," said Bobby. "We're the best friends you'll ever have. Do you know how long eternity is?"

"What kind of a loaded question is that?"

"So you tried and now you're tired," he said. "Oh, the pity of it.

When are you going to get your head out of your ass and stop feeling sorry for yourself?"

"Is that all you think this is?"

"Everybody's got a sad story, Slick," said Frenchie. "We heard yours already."

"I'm not going to say you owe us anything," said Bobby, "You took the same chance we did. But we don't have a voice anymore. We're dead. You're not. You do."

"So?" I said.

"So use it," he said.